Reflection
Recognition
Reaffirmation

An Engaging Frame of Reference
for Leisure Education
2nd Edition

Jeff Witman, Ed.D., CTRS

Mary Ligon, Ph.D., CTRS

Foreword by Sharon Nichols

Idyll Arbor, Inc.

39129 264th Ave SE, Enumclaw, WA 98022 (360) 825-7797

Idyll Arbor Editor: Thomas M. Blaschko

ISBN: 9781882883738

Printed in the United States of America

Contents

Foreword v

Preface ix

Acknowledgements xiii

Helpful Hints 1

Reflection 3

Recognition 41

Reaffirmation 81

Social Skills 111

Stress Management 143

Senior Activities.. 163

Assessment 183

Program Development.. 189

Program Examples 197

A Final Thought.. 219

References 223

Activity List

10 THINGS TO DO WITH "10 THINGS I LOVE TO DO"...67

20 (OR SO) QUESTIONS..119

21 LEISURELY QUESTIONS..26

A GIFT TO MYSELF: MANAGING HOLIDAY STRESS...153

A POTPOURRI OF GOALS...89

A POTPOURRI OF SOCIAL NEEDS..113

ABOUT NOTHING...5

ACCORDING TO SARAH PALIN..108

ACTIVITY PIE...11

AMISH EVENING..53

ATTITUDES...109

A-Z..134

BEEN THERE, DONE THAT: MAXIMIZING THE POSITIVE DURING TIMES OF TRANSITIONS.........177

BOXES...87

BUMMER SCALE..48

CAN'T GET THERE FROM HERE...50

CIRCLE TALK..101

COMPANY PICNIC..42

CONTINUUM...140

CONTRACT...93

COOPERATION AND TRUST SCALE..126

COULDA SHOULDA WOULDA..84

CRUISING...73

CRYSTAL BALL: MAKING THE MOST OF YOUR RETIREMENT YEARS......................175

DID PICASSO HAVE THE RIGHT IDEA?..102

DREAMS AND SCHEMES..124

EMOTIONAL LOTTO!!...122

FAITH MATTERS OR MATTERS OF FAITH..79

FAMILY CONNECTIONS...6

FEELINGS MENU..137

FEELINGS...69

G.A.S...85

GLORY DAYS..9

GOING FOR THE BURN...62

HAVE YOU EVER…..34

HURRY UP!..103

I SEE FROM WHERE I STAND..78

IDEAL DREAM VACATION...30

IN THE FLOW..46

INTERVIEWS...29

INTRODUCTION INTERVIEWS...117

JUDGING TIME...4

L.I.F.E. (Leisure Is Fabulously Exciting)...75

LAUGH-THINK-CRY..65

LEISURE 10 QUESTIONS...17

LEISURE COAT OF ARMS...170

LEISURE INDEX: RECREATION ROLODEX...86

LEISURE MAP...15

LEISURE OUTBURST...21

LEISURE SHOW AND TELL..164

LEISURE SWAP...72

LEISURE TIMELINE CONTINUUM...31

LIFESTYLE CHECKLIST..13
LIFESTYLE COACHES...76
LOOKING AHEAD...82
LOW AND NO-COST...91
MAGIC WAND..99
MATCHING..10
MEETINGS AND GREETINGS...115
MY LEISURE STRESSORS...161
MY WISH LIST...181
NEEDS vs. ACTIVITIES..58
NO-DISCOUNT CONTRACT..95
ON MOTIVATION...54
ON NEEDS..56
ON SEIZING THE MOMENT...97
PAY TO PLAY...39
PERFECT DAY..158
PERFECT GET-A-WAY..8
PET PEEVES..66
PICTURES..37
POSITIVE ASSERTIONS..133
POSITIVE SELF-TALK: IS THE GLASS HALF EMPTY OR HALF FULL?.................................155
PRECIOUS TIME...64
PRESCRIPTION FOR MANAGING MY STRESS..149
PROGRESSIVE MUSCLE RELAXATION..159
REACTIONS TO STRESS CIIECKLIST...144
REPORT CARD...60
RETIREMENT PLANS..24
RIGHT STUFF..135
ROLES IN GROUPS..131
ROOM..40
SIMON SAYS..52
SOME OF US…...36
SOME UNIQUE PEOPLE...128
SOURCES OF STRESS..146
STRETCHING YOUR WAY TO RELAXATION..160
SUCCESSFUL AGING...173
SURVEY...139
TIE THAT BINDS...179
TREE...104
VIEW-ER CLUE-ER DO-ER..130
WELLNESS PERSPECTIVES..106
WHAT'S KEEPING ME FROM HAVING FUN?..44
WHEREVER YOU GO, THERE YOU ARE…..167
WHO ARE YOU?...165
WHO SAID IT..141
WOULD YOU RATHER HAVE?..70
YOU MAKE THE CALL...33

Foreword

It is an honor to provide the forward to this publication. Dr. Jeff Witman and Dr. Mary Ligon have seen evolutionary and revolutionary changes in health care service delivery. They continue to explore the importance of leisure in relation to the health care arena. Both Dr. Witman and Dr. Ligon are "seasoned" practitioners whose experiences are linked to actual practice as well as educating others about the practice of therapeutic recreation/recreational therapy. Combined they have decades of direct "hands on" experience as well as research and academic experiences. The exercises in this book are rooted in practice.

Models have come, models have gone, but the core fundamentals of practice still exist and survive despite the cacophony of philosophies that have emerged over time. Leisure is a core fundamental to our practice. Another essential element of therapeutic recreation/recreational therapy practice is that the people with whom we work are in need of some type of change in their lives. It is true not only of humans, but also of any species, that survival is ultimately linked to the ability to adapt to and adjust to change.

The core elements of *Reflection, Recognition, and Reaffirmation* are closely aligned with models of change that are used across not only the health care spectrum but in all aspects of business, industry, and technology. As noted in the book, the first step for creating change is Reflection (contemplating the what). It is conceptualizing that change needs to occur and seeking the knowledge, skills, and abilities that are required in order to accommodate/adjust for the change that is desired. Without change, one just exists. In contemplating change, one begins to identify and realize that there is choice available. It helps a person understand that there are possibilities and outcomes as to what can be or how one can be engaged in living in a meaningful way.

The Recognition stage heralds the opportunity to explore new behaviors, to face some of the challenges that may be barriers to change, and to use the tools that will be instrumental in building one's efficacy for change.

Finally, the stage of Reaffirmation is the level at which one integrates change as a lifelong strength and ability. It is the level at which a person can say out loud that this is who I am seeking to be and continue to affirm that outcomes have been achieved so that he or she can continue to live a life of possibilities.

This revised edition is long overdue. The original version was the starting point for change. This second edition capitalizes on what was best in the first volume but now brings in the changes that are needed for this to continue to be a dynamic publication. There are some new exercises as well as some "tried and true" ones. There are additional perspectives as to how we might assist some specific populations. (The Baby Boomers are getting older!) Bottom line and what has always been true even in the first version is that leisure is an important element of living and, especially, a significant aspect of living well.

Practitioners need to consider this publication, in its second edition, as a vehicle that continues to be a catalyst to enable people to move forward with life and to become the change that they want to see in themselves.

Sharon Nichols, CTRS/L
Northeast Area Clinical Specialist — Therapeutic Recreation
Genesis Health Care Corporation

Preface

You can discover more about a person in an hour of play
than in a year of conversation.

— Plato

Thoughts from Jeff

As a graduate at the University of Oregon in the mid-1970s, I had a first-hand view of the enthusiasm generated by Chet McDowell and others for the concept and practice of leisure counseling. Practitioners and students were thrilled with the idea of transcending the activity leader role and becoming "real" therapists. Educators and academicians reveled in a novel field for their philosophizing and model building. Debates raged on esoteric paradigms such as "Leisure Education vs. Leisure Counseling." Workshops were held. Books were written. Program models were tried. Assessments were deified. Assessments were demystified. Assessments were thrown in the can. When the dust settled, or at least cleared away a bit, some understandings emerged for many individuals actually doing (as opposed to proselytizing about) leisure education programs. These included the realizations that leisure education:

- is not a panacea for people's problems;

- has a differential impact based on many environmental, client, and leader factors;

- requires a goodness of fit between participant needs and program strategies;

- defies the cookie-cutter or one-curriculum-for-all approach; and

- is augmented when supported by peers or significant others.

The sequential approach (reflection — recognition — reaffirmation) utilized in organizing this book reflects typical practice in programming. First, participants are engaged in experiences that encourage them to consider leisure as something with unique meanings to them. Next, they're involved in activities that allow for some clarification of the role of leisure in their lives. Finally, participants are asked to consider where they want to go with what they've learned about themselves. Table 1 provides some of the expectations for leisure education inherent in this model. The decision to change or stay the same is thus based on some measure of thoughtfulness. Participants' investment in such decisions transcends that of the intuitive New Year's resolution or the hastily conceived promise to oneself. This sequence of considerations is analogous to the sequence of processing suggested by Project Adventure in their training materials: "What? So What? Now What?"

Reflection (What?)

- reflects upon leisure as a distinct component of the life experience

- reflects on the impact of leisure upon individuals and groups

- reflects upon the various conceptualizations and perspectives of leisure

Recognition (So What?)

- recognizes relationship of personal needs and leisure potentials

- recognizes potential resources for fulfillment through leisure

- recognizes barriers to leisure fulfillment

Reaffirmation (Now What?)

- reaffirms goals for future leisure

- reaffirms benefits/payoffs for accomplishment of goals

- develops a plan for accomplishing goals

Table 1: Examples from the Reflection — Recognition — Reaffirmation Continuum

Counseling is purposely not a part of the title of this booklet or of the approaches suggested. It is our contention that counseling is best left to counselors. We prefer to say education, in that the principles of quality education for adults (collaborative planning, respect for "learned experience" of participants, emphasis on processing and support) are ideal for leisure education. Facilitators of leisure education programs need not be gurus, only empathetic fellow pursuers of satisfying lifestyles. Their expertise should lie in creating thoughtful, creative exercises and environments for self-directed exploration, not in prescribing omnipotent dictums to be memorized and applied.

"Transitions" has become a buzzword in human services with concern directed at helping people deal with change. These transitions include things like moving from hospitals to communities, adjusting to aging or disability, coping with the loss of job or of loved ones and so forth. The commonality of transitions for human service providers is that they all provide opportunities to provide service recipients (to paraphrase the adage) with the ability and equipment to catch fish or with the seafood platter. The latter approach implies continued dependence. The former suggests an ideal for the development and implementation of leisure education programs — namely that participants in such programs acquire attitudes of self-empowerment regarding their leisure and tools for self-help that are reusable. Shift happens, and well-conceived leisure education programs can help people deal with it!

I believe that the thoughts and exercises in this book can assist in this challenging process. They have worked with all of the people we have worked with at least some of the time, and with some of the people we have worked with all the time! They are good ideas and have been field tested for several decades with a wide variety of populations. Without doubt, though, they will get better through your adaptations and variations, which will reflect the unique skills of you and the people you work with. Kunstler and Daly (2010, p.164) contend that "leisure education can be tailored to the needs and functioning level of just about any client, his family, or the service setting." I think they are right and would add the notion that customizing the way you design and present programs will enhance their relevance and effectiveness.

A few notes on this second edition are in order. Mary Ligon is the co-author and has added perspectives on stress management and on seniors. We've added many new activities, updated the assessment and reference information, and, thanks to the folks at Idyll Arbor, developed a new look to the publication.

Thoughts from Mary

I was first introduced to the concept of leisure education as an undergraduate at Radford University. It was 1984, and Peterson and Gunn's text, *Therapeutic Recreation Program Design: Principles and Procedures*, was only in its second edition. This was my first introduction to the Leisure Ability Model. I was on the cusp of becoming a professional, full of excitement and vigor. I was fascinated with the prospect of being a Recreation Therapist and having tools to help people receive full benefit from their own leisure involvement. Being the product of two educators, the leisure education category of the Leisure Ability Model was particularly appealing to me. I thought that the idea of leisure being beneficial to one's health and well-being would be a self-evident truth, that it would be a popular idea with clients and other professionals alike. I thought leisure education would primarily entail teaching the needed skills and providing adequate resources to clients. To my surprise, the Puritan work ethic turned out to be alive and well in many instances. Therefore, leisure awareness was a much bigger piece of this process than I had anticipated.

Through years of hands on experience with clients, I found that understanding ourselves and the contributions that leisure involvement can make in our lives, in good times and bad, is a key piece in the leisure education process. As a gerontologist, I've also learned that acquisition of self-awareness is not a one-time endeavor. As we age, we develop and change as does the meaning and function of leisure in our lives. The fifth edition, by Stumbo and Peterson, became available in 2008, and the Leisure Ability Model still stands. This model, which places Leisure Education in a transitional position between the functional intervention and recreation participation, has provided professionals in the field of therapeutic recreation with a framework for service provision. I hope that the exercises included in this book will serve as practical tools for those implementing leisure education programs with clients of all ages.

Acknowledgements

Mary Strickler Sarver, my great aunt, served in the American Red Cross Recreation Service during and after World War II. Whenever I thought I had a new activity, I'd share it with her and the majority of the time she could identify a previous version of what I'd imagined was a seminal thought! Many of the activities in this text have, I'm sure, been seen before so I'll try to identify and recognize some sources with full knowledge that there probably are other or older roots to some of them. Sincere thanks to:

All of the folks involved with the first edition of this book — Jennifer Kurtz, Karen Taylor, and Sharon Nichols in particular — have ideas and activities reflected in the new edition.

Kathleen Marged for her booklet *Many Moves for a Healthier Lifestyle*, which included versions of "What's Keeping Me from Having Fun," "Leisure 10 Questions," and "Leisure Outburst." Earlier versions of these appear in McDowell and in Stumbo and Thompson.

Leandra Bedini for the "Magic Wand" activity.

Rhonda Booth for the concepts involved with "Attitudes" and "The Tree" and her colleague at Capital Health, Jacqueline Cook, for the sample program information. All the folks I got to work with at Capital Health (Adrienne, Emily, Cheryl, Kathy, Andrea, Bernadine, Crystal, Lukas, Shannon, and Mandy) were committed to leisure education and passionate about promoting leisure and well being.

Norma Stumbo and colleagues for previous versions of "The Room," "The Tree," and "Leisure Coat of Arms" and for a series of fantastic activity booklets which spawned a variety of spin-off activities.

Helen Finch for the "Lifestyle Checklist."

Dean Zoerink for a version of "Pictures."

Angela Vauter for her vision of what community reintegration should be.

Lynn Anderson and Linda Heyne for the content/concepts associated with the "Components of Well Being Scale."

Project Adventure, Inc. for versions of many of the initiatives and games included with the social skills information.

Colleagues at Hampstead Hospital, Philhaven Behavioral Health, and the No Longer Alone Ministries for their adaptations and tweaks with many of the activities. Co-leaders with leisure education and social skills groups who taught me a lot include Erlinde, Deb, Mike, Kelly, Ida, Dennis, and Mary.

Helpful Hints

This book is designed to be useful in a variety of settings. As such, each type of setting, each agency, and each group of clients will be different. Therefore, you will need to tailor activities in order to get the most "bang for your buck." However, guidelines are provided for each activity that should prove to be helpful. For each of the activities included, three components are listed: 1) Goal, 2) Format, and 3) Processing. Here are some hints for utilizing this information as well as considerations on group size, timing, formations, and materials that may be needed. While most activities are described for groups, many of the activities can also be effective components of 1:1 work with clients.

Goal: You will notice that each activity has an overarching goal. The goal will give you a broad perspective of what you can expect clients/patients to gain from completing the exercise. As you develop therapeutic recreation programs, it is important to assess the global mission of the agency you work for, the mission of your department, and, most importantly, to assess clients' needs. You may find that activities in the "Recognition" section can be of assistance in assessing these needs. It is also important to assess clients' readiness to work in groups, and to determine where the group is in terms of ability to share openly and work cooperatively. Sequencing of activities is always an important consideration and can help promote group cohesion.

Completing a thorough assessment in advance will help you to create and structure programs that will be of greatest benefit to your consumers. As you familiarize yourself with activities listed in this book, aim to select ones that 1) support programmatic goals, 2) fit with the group's current dynamics, and 3) aid clients/patients in acquisition of leisure awareness, knowledge, and skills. The goal listed for each activity provides the therapist with guidance in selecting activities that will be congruent with programmatic goals and will best meet clients' needs.

Format: Each activity includes a section on format. Here you will find a description of how the activity is designed to be implemented. Most activities require a writing surface and writing utensils. Most also require making copies of handouts for participants. On a few occasions, you will note that other articles/supplies are needed. The format section is short so that you can easily identify what, if any, special materials are needed. It is usually best to set up a room so that all group members can see one another and have equal access to interacting with others. A circle set-up is usually best, and having clients sitting in rows facing forward (classroom style) is not likely to encourage interaction. Each setting provides its own unique set-up benefits and challenges, so experiment until you find what works best given the options that you have.

Another consideration for implementation is group size. For the most part, activities in this text are designed to be implemented in a small group setting of 4-12 participants. Nearly all can be adapted for one-on-one interventions as well. When working with groups, keep in the mind that you will need enough clients to provide energy to make the group interesting and enough staff to provide support that clients may need. It is usually best to limit the group to 12 participants so that everyone has enough face time. In some cases, your groups may need to be much smaller, depending on the amount of assistance clients need. In selecting group members, remember that variety is the spice of life — having 12 very outgoing members will present one challenge while including 12 shy individuals will result in another. Balance the need for variety with the need to be able to relate to others and share commonalities.

Consider the timing of activities within the context of the environment in which you work. The amount of time required for each activity will vary depending on your clientele. You may want to ask yourself the following questions: Will I see my clients frequently over a course of weeks or months? Or will they be discharged in a matter of days? Will I have sufficient time to complete and process the activity with clients in one session or do I need multiple sessions? Will I need to combine or break up the activity with a more active pursuit? Will a break time be necessary? Is this an open group where different clients might attend each session? Or is this a closed group in which the same group members will be together each time? Answers to these questions will help you select the most appropriate activities.

Processing: The discussion that follows an activity can be as important and helpful as the activity itself. Therefore, a section on "Processing" is provided for each activity. Here you will find questions that help clients articulate what they learned through completing the activity. When clients are able to articulate lessons learned, they are more likely to take ownership of their thoughts and insights, more so than if they simply record thoughts on paper without sharing them. At the same time, it is important to respect clients' comfort level in sharing their thoughts and feelings. Create a safe and comfortable environment in which one might feel comfortable sharing, but don't coerce. The amount of time you will need to allot for processing the activity will vary according to clients' needs and abilities.

Before you select an activity, a quick review of this checklist may be helpful. Remember the rule of thumb, "Measure twice, and cut once." This old adage can help you in the workshop and when working with people.

Check List:

☐ Does the goal of the activity match programmatic and client goals?

☐ Do I need to do some warm-ups to get clients ready to participate?

☐ Have I created a safe and comfortable environment?

☐ Do I need special materials in addition to handouts, writing utensils, and a writing surface?

☐ Have I carefully considered who would benefit from participating in this activity and the best mix of group members?

☐ Is the room set up in a way that promotes social interaction and equality?

☐ Do I have enough time to complete the activity in one session? If not, can I realistically schedule a follow-up meeting?

☐ Have I reviewed the processing section? Am I prepared to lead a discussion?

Reflection

Not everything that is faced can be changed, but nothing can be changed until it is faced.

— *James Baldwin*

Being asked to reflect can be difficult! Sometimes the thought, let alone any insight, just isn't there. So you come up with something that sounds reasonably good for the question posed and you survive your turn to share, but the exercise itself has little impact for you. Inevitably though, if the exercise has been a thoughtful one, it comes to mind again at a time when you can truly be reflective and your response to it becomes real, meaningful, cathartic even. For this reason "Reflection" exercises need to be an ongoing component of leisure education programming. Rather than simply using one at the start of programs to "break the ice," consider infusing them into each program segment. This allows an opportunity for sharing the reflection that is done away from the leisure education program and integrating it into the participant's work on "Recognition" and "Reaffirmation." It is good to remember, too, that individual triggers for reflection vary, and that increasing the number and variety of "Reflection" exercises will enhance the breadth and depth of a participant's reflections.

JUDGING TIME

GOAL

To reflect upon the accuracy with which we judge the time of our lives.

FORMAT

Participants are given the following challenge:

Let's see how good a judge of time you are. I'll say "begin" and when you think a minute has gone by stand up. Ready? Begin.

Wait until everyone is standing, then let participants know the times of the first and last person to stand and also who was closest to a minute. (Perhaps a prize for them.)

PROCESSING

Begin with the thought that few of us are totally accurate in judging the "time" of our lives — that while we may be correct saying we've got no time for leisure, in fact it may just be that the fragments of daily "free" time we possess only makes it seem that way. With time awareness and management might come more usable blocks of time for leisure.

ABOUT NOTHING

GOAL

To reflect upon the relationship of time and leisure.

FORMAT

Begin with the thought that as kids we often answered our parents' question, "What have you been doing all day?" with "Nothing." Sometimes it was because we had been doing something we didn't want them to know about, but often it was because we really couldn't remember exactly how our day had progressed. We had experienced, certainly without intellectualizing about it, a sense of timelessness. We went out in the morning, and the next thing we knew it was getting dark and the dinner bell was ringing. Have each participant list at least three activities or experiences in each of the columns below.

HIGHLY CONSCIOUS OF TIME   **UNAWARE OF TIME**

_____   _____

_____   _____

_____   _____

_____   _____

_____   _____

PROCESSING

Depending on the needs of the group, this exercise can turn toward a discussion of time management and the various self-assessment instruments (e.g., time budget, pie-of-life), or move toward discussion of leisure as a state of mind — freedom, intrinsic motivation — and how this relates to our awareness of time

FAMILY CONNECTIONS

GOAL

To recognize leisure patterns within family systems.

FORMAT

Participants are asked to generate a collage of pictures that includes an area for each family member's leisure interests as well as sections that show activities various combinations of the family enjoy. Include a section that represents what the family does all together.

A section for anticipated future activities can also be included.

Non-traditional family patterns can be utilized if they are more appropriate for participants; friends are certainly another approach to the exercise. One possible layout would be

Dad	Mom
Dad and Children — **Whole Family**	**Mom and Children**
Participant	Sibling(s)

PROCESSING

Discussion can center upon needs/problems/strengths the exercise identifies (e.g., what are some things whole families can do?). Another approach is to do a diagram (see Leisure Loves, which follows) including activities the various combinations of family members participate in. Ask participants to identify activities their families participate in for each of the areas of the diagram.

Leisure Loves

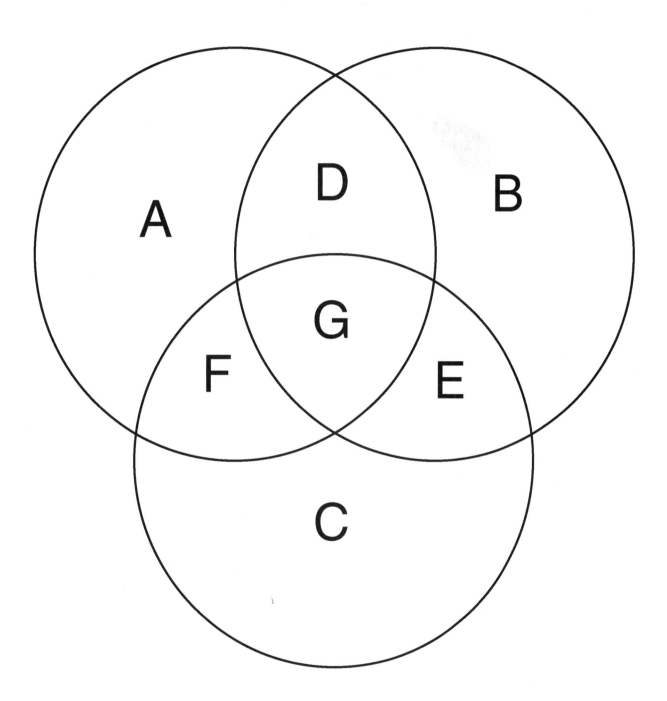

A. Dad only   **B.** Mom only   **C.** Child only   **D.** Mom and Dad

E. Mom and Child   **F.** Dad and Child   **G.** All three

THE PERFECT GET-A-WAY

GOAL

To relate leisure ideals with practical realities.

FORMAT

Participants fill in the blanks in the following scenario:

THE GET-A-WAY

WOW! I can't believe it! _____

without having to worry about work. My bags are packed, _____

here I come! I should really say "we" because _____

is coming along, too. I can hardly wait to _____.

After that there will be time for _____,

_____,

and _____.

The beauty of it is that I won't have to worry about _____

and _____,

and there won't be any _____

there.

PROCESSING

After sharing their "get-a-way," participants are asked to describe how any of this might become a part of their real worlds — on a daily, weekly, monthly, perhaps yearly basis. Can you get-a-way without really getting away?

GLORY DAYS

GOAL

To identify enjoyed leisure experiences from the past.

FORMAT

Participants listen to Bruce Springsteen's "Glory Days" and are asked to identify their own glory days.

A more mellow song — "Those Were the Days," "The Way We Were," etc., may be more appropriate for a more mellow group.

PROCESSING

Ask the questions

- What was it that made them so special?

- Can any of this be realized now?

A timeline of leisure highlights of the past can complement this. So can three leisure highlights from various developmental periods.

MATCHING

GOAL

To identify personal leisure preferences and recognize the preferences of others.

FORMAT

Select someone to be the first leader of the group or lead the first round of the activity yourself. The leader selects three personal leisure interests and demonstrates a motion for each. For example:

Texting — frantic movement of fingers on an imaginary keyboard

Reading — form "book" with hands and move head from side to side

Poker — pretend to shuffle and deal cards

The group then forms a circle with all members facing away from the center of the circle.

Action is initiated by the leader saying "ready" then "reveal."

On hearing "reveal" the group turns quickly toward the center. Each participant initiates one of the three activity motions as they turn.

Those who happen to select the same movement selected by the leader survive to another round.

Last one eliminated is the new leader.

PROCESSING

Have participants generate a motion for an activity they would like to try in the future. See if others can guess what the activity is.

ACTIVITY PIE

GOAL

To assess range and character of present leisure involvement.

FORMAT

PIE SLICES. Using the pie diagram on the next page, fill in a portion of the pie equal to your participation in a particular activity type:

0 = not a part of my lifestyle
¼ = occasional part of my lifestyle
½ = regular part of my lifestyle
¾ = major part of my lifestyle
Fully Shaded = most important part of my lifestyle

PROCESSING

Slides with pictures of examples of each activity group can be helpful to the validity of this exercise. Follow-up questions might focus on:

- areas you want to see increased

- areas you want to see decreased

- single most important change the exercise suggests

Pie Slices

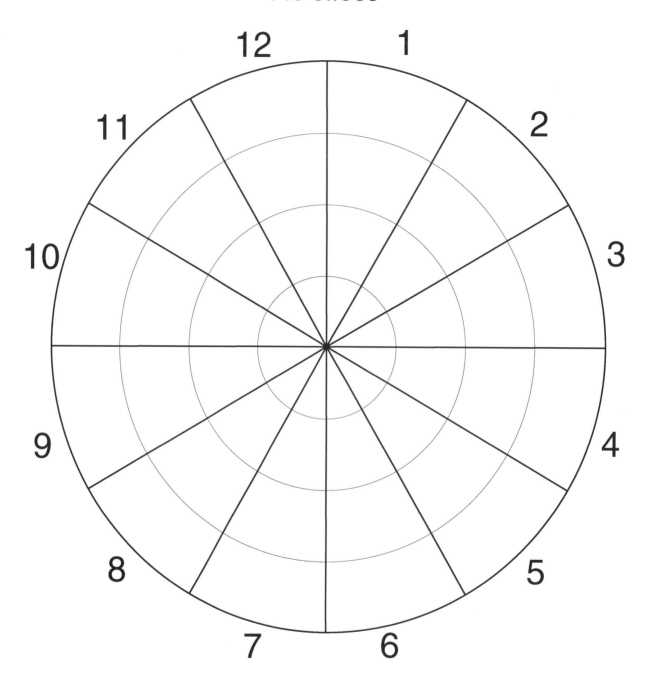

1 = games
2 = sports
3 = nature activities
4 = collection activities
5 = craft activities
6 = art & music activities

7 = volunteer/organizational activities
8 = religious/spiritual activities
9 = educational & cultural activities
10 = romance & sex
11 = drugs and/or alcohol
12 = gambling

LIFESTYLE CHECKLIST

GOAL

To assess personal performance in a variety of characteristics and behaviors related to lifestyle.

FORMAT

Have the participants review the statements on the next page and fill in the blanks to say whether they are or are not doing the activity described.

Tell them to consider possible changes in lifestyle that might improve their lives.

PROCESSING

Allow individuals to identify the statement they're least pleased with and reflect upon needed changes.

Lifestyle Checklist

As you review the statements below, consider how well you are performing relative to each of them. Fill in a "yes" or a "no" in each blank. Furthermore, if your answers are not satisfactory to you, consider what changes in your lifestyle might be required.

I am or am not:

_____ 1. exercising rigorously no less than twenty minutes at least three times per week.

_____ 2. keeping my BMI (Body Mass Index) number under 25.

_____ 3. achieving a good balance between work, play, and relaxation.

_____ 4. having a sincere, positive, caring relationship with at least one other person.

_____ 5. having a positive sense of community with at least one group of people whom I am in close and frequent contact.

_____ 6. demonstrating breadth (a minimum of three interests) and balance (both active and passive activities, both group and solitary activities) in my leisure pursuits.

_____ 7. recognizing and taking advantage of community resources (recreation departments, Y's, churches, etc.) for leisure.

_____ 8. overcoming barriers to leisure participation (insufficient time, skills, or funds) and coping with leisure related problems (boredom, guilt, and compulsiveness).

_____ 9. continually reflecting upon my leisure needs and making and carrying out plans toward better meeting these needs.

_____ 10. in agreement with the statement, "We don't stop playing because we grow old; we grow old because we stop playing."

LEISURE MAP

GOAL

To prioritize leisure interests and relate them to personal needs.

FORMAT

Participants complete the "Best Day for Me" exercise on the next page. Their scores are computed and interpreted.

PROCESSING

Ideal for introducing the thought that breadth and balance in a lifestyle can be positive influences. Also typically leads into the realization that an activity can be used in many ways.

Also useful in this regard is the Optimist/Pessimist story in which a child who is an incurable optimist and another child who is an incurable pessimist are brought to a psychologist.

The psychologist fills an observation room with toys for the pessimist. The child enters, looks around, and begins to cry saying, "No way I can play with all of these" and "They're nice now but some day they'll break."

For the optimist the room is filled with manure, which she seems to really enjoy. She digs in the stuff and generally has a great time. The psychologist can't understand her happiness and comes into the room to ask her how she possibly could be smiling. Her reply, "Well, with all this manure I know there's a pony in here somewhere!"

The point is that state of mind will determine what the activity will be.

THE BEST DAY FOR ME

1. Bookstore browsing, daydreaming, doing crosswords

2. Meditation, listening to music, reading

3. Making things, letter writing, gardening

4. Treadmill, swimming, journal writing

5. Going to an amusement park, watching TV with others, visiting flea market

6. Going to a party, hanging out with supportive friends, visiting family

7. Giving massage, playing with kids, volunteer work

8. Playing cards, bowling, gambling, racetrack

Choose (circle) one from each pair of activities:

1 or 2	2 or 3	3 or 4	4 or 5	5 or 6	6 or 7	7 or 8
1 or 3	2 or 4	3 or 5	4 or 6	5 or 7	6 or 8	
1 or 4	2 or 5	3 or 6	4 or 7	5 or 8		
1 or 5	2 or 6	3 or 7	4 or 8			
1 or 6	2 or 7	3 or 8				
1 or 7	2 or 8					
1 or 8						

Add up the number of times you circled each number:

1 = _____   2 = _____   3 = _____   4 = _____   5= _____   6 = _____   7 = _____   8 = _____

SOLITUDE =   *1 + 2 + 3 + 4 =* _____

RELATED TO OTHERS =   *5 + 6 + 7 + 8 =* _____

SPECTATOR =   *1 + 2 + 5 + 6 =* _____

PARTICIPANT =   *3 + 4 + 7 + 8 =* _____

LEISURE 10 QUESTIONS

GOAL

To identify characteristics of various leisure activities.

FORMAT

Can be structured as an individual or a team challenge. Leader reads the clues and participants try to identify the activity being described. Sets of questions are shown below.

PROCESSING

Have participants develop a five-statement sequence for an activity that they know well and share it with the group. An alternative is to have participants research an activity that they would like to learn more about and generate a five- or ten-statement list.

PINOCHLE

1. I can be played by two or three or four people at one time.
2. There are many rules to know in order to play.
3. Marriages are common in me.
4. If four people are playing, we have partners.
5. "Meld" gives you points at the beginning of the game.
6. My deck of cards is not the same as other decks.
7. Having the Queen of Spades and the Jack of Diamonds is not worth much, but if you have both Queens and Jacks, you had better bid high!
8. Opening bid is 21.
9. The lowest card in my deck is 9.
10. If three people play, the winner of the bid gets to play the "Widow's Hand."

ICE SKATING

1. I can be done alone or with others.
2. It takes a bit of coordination to do me.
3. I can be done inside or outside.
4. I am an event in the Winter Olympics.
5. People of all ages enjoy me.
6. Better dress warmly if you plan to do me.
7. You can buy or rent the only equipment needed to do me.
8. Some people buy fancy outfits to do me.
9. I think I'm fun, but many people still avoid me.
10. To be of use, you need to do me at least three times a week, doing aerobic type stuff.

EXERCISE

1. I can be done anywhere, any time.
2. Anybody can do this (some may need to adapt).
3. Many people like to go special places to do me.
4. I can be very expensive or not — it depends on you.
5. I can require a lot of equipment — or not.
6. Some people do me while they watch the television.
7. I can make you feel better — both physically and mentally.
8. Some people buy fancy outfits to do me.
9. I think I'm fun, but many people still avoid me.
10. To be of use, you need to do me at least three times a week, doing aerobic type stuff.

MACRAMÉ

1. I can be done by people about 10 and older.
2. I do cost money, but it is stretched out over time.
3. I am usually done at home.
4. You can teach yourself, or have someone else teach you.
5. I can be very simple or very complex.
6. I was very popular during the 1960s.
7. Fishermen are responsible for creating me.
8. I can be helpful in loosening up stiff fingers.
9. You tie me up in knots.
10. When I am finished, most people let me hold their plants.

CROQUET

1. I am played outside.
2. I originated in "Olde Englande."
3. My game uses colorful balls.
4. You have to know rules to play me.
5. You have to buy special equipment to play me.
6. People of different ages can play together.
7. Usually I only have enough for six or eight to play.
8. You have to lay me out in a special arrangement to play me.
9. Sometimes you get to hit another player's ball as far as you can.
10. The first one back to the beginning wins.

CHARADES

1. All you need to play me is a good imagination.
2. I am most commonly played by teams.
3. When I was originally invented in France in the 18th century, I was more like a riddle.
4. After World War II, I became what I am now — some called me "The Game."
5. The team that guesses the right answer first wins.
6. People take turns being the "designated actor."
7. Nowadays, movie, book, or television titles are the mystery.
8. Not allowed to use inanimate objects.
9. I can be played by almost everybody.
10. No talking allowed.

READING

1. I am most commonly done alone; however, it's not necessarily always the case.
2. I am something that almost everybody does — some more than others.
3. I can be done practically anywhere.
4. In order to do me, you can either buy or borrow me.
5. Long ago, it used to be that only priests and scholars could do me.
6. The material inside me is as diverse as the people who do me.
7. I can have pictures.
8. There are some people who have never acquired the skill to do me — but it's never too late.
9. I can become very expensive if you buy me and do me frequently.
10. If you are blind, there are special adaptations.

WALKING

1. I can be done anywhere.
2. I can be done alone or with others.
3. You should buy a good pair of _____ to do me.
4. I can be done with a friend.
5. I can be done fast or slow.
6. Some use me for a form of exercise.
7. When the weather is not cooperating, I can be done inside.
8. I can be relaxing to some.
9. The only cost is the good pair of _____.
10. Running would be to do me too quickly.

BACKGAMMON

1. You need at least two people to do me.
2. Acey Deucy is another version of me.
3. I have a doubling cube, but this was a modern addition to me.
4. I am a one-time cost, but that cost can vary.
5. Although I look easy to play, I have some complicated rules to learn.
6. Choette is another version of me that allows three or more to play.
7. In playing me, you need to learn the terms — bar, blot, escape, pips, and more.
8. The player who gets all of his "men" off the board first wins.
9. Taking your "men" off the board is called 'bearing off.'
10. It is believed that I was first played by the Romans as early as 3000 BC.

BICYCLING

1. I can be done inside or outside.
2. The first one of me was invented in 1645, but it didn't look like I look now.
3. Some people use me to race.
4. I come in different colors and sizes.
5. There is a large initial investment plus maintenance fees.
6. I can be done for sport, recreation, or transportation.
7. I can come with one or two or three or many_____.
8. Special ones of me can be made to accommodate more than one at a time.
9. "Daisy" had to use me when she got married.
10. When first learning to do me, some use training _____.

GEOCACHING

1. Nearly a million sites around the world.
2. There's a "Complete Idiot's Guide" to it.
3. Base maps can be helpful.
4. Started in 2000.
5. Benchmarks can be part of it.
6. Groundspeak is associated with it.
7. Logbooks are at each site.
8. A modern day treasure hunt.
9. You need a GPS to participate.
10. Third syllable sounds like something done with checks.

LEISURE OUTBURST

GOAL

To identify examples of different categories of activities.

FORMAT

Can be a group or an individual challenge to see if all ten of the examples in a category can be named in a certain amount of time, e.g., one minute.

PROCESSING

Working with a partner, have participants generate lists related to the area they live in and leisure/recreation. For example, pizza places, natural wonders, unusual buildings, trails.

Have them share them with the group.

An alternative is to generate lists of common leisure challenges, for example, games to keep a long car ride interesting or no-cost activities.

CARD GAMES

1. Pinochle
2. Bridge
3. Hearts
4. Poker
5. Uno
6. Euchre
7. Rummy
8. Canasta
9. Solitaire
10. War

TABLE GAMES

1. Monopoly
2. Cards
3. Backgammon
4. Chess
5. Checkers
6. Scrabble
7. Parcheesi
8. Trivial Pursuit
9. Yahtzee
10. Sorry

VIDEO GAMES

1. Super Smash Brothers
2. Guitar Hero
3. World of Warcraft
4. Grand Theft Auto
5. Halo
6. Madden
7. Super Mario Brothers
8. Wii sports
9. Tetris
10. The Sims

SOLITARY GAMES/ACTIVITIES

1. Reading
2. Watching TV
3. Solitaire
4. Painting/drawing
5. Crossword puzzles
6. Listening to music
7. Sewing
8. Baking/cooking
9. Writing letters
10. Crafts/hobbies

OUTSIDE ACTIVITIES

1. Croquet
2. Gardening
3. Walking
4. Horse shoes
5. Bocce
6. Sunbathing
7. Badminton
8. Volleyball
9. Swimming
10. Bicycling

HOBBIES/CRAFTS

1. Needlepoint
2. Knitting/crochet
3. Woodworking
4. Macramé
5. Collections (any)
6. Stained glass windows
7. Tole painting
8. Scrapbooking
9. Bonsai plants
10. Calligraphy

EXERCISES

1. Yoga
2. Aerobics
3. Weight lifting
4. Bicycling
5. Rowing machines
6. Jumping rope
7. Swimming
8. Walking
9. Jogging
10. Sit-ups

RETIREMENT PLANS

GOAL

To identify popular activities for retirement.

FORMAT

Working individually, participants are asked to rank the activities that follow.

The first challenge is to rank the activities by popularity among current retirees. 1 = most popular through 10 = least popular.

The second challenge is to rank the activities by amount spent on them. 1 = most expensive through 10 = least expensive.

The third activity is for the participants to rank the activities by how much they want to do each one. 1 = most desirable through 10 = least desirable.

PROCESSING

Have participants share their top choice(s) and identify where they see themselves doing them and who they will be doing them with. The same list is used for three alternative activities. Participants can attempt to match the ranks of the items by popularity or by average amount spent on them. Correct answers for the first two challenges are

Popularity: a, h, e, b, j, g, c, f, i, d

Amount spent: a, j, g, c, e, d, h, b, f, i

Using the third ranking, participants can see how their preferences match with the preferences of other members of the group and retirees in general.

Retirement Choices

Activity	popularity	expense	personal choice
a. Traveling	_____	_____	_____
b. Reading	_____	_____	_____
c. Fishing	_____	_____	_____
d. Family Activities	_____	_____	_____
e. Home Improvement	_____	_____	_____
f. Volunteering	_____	_____	_____
g. Hobbies	_____	_____	_____
h. Golfing	_____	_____	_____
i. Exercising	_____	_____	_____
j. Gardening	_____	_____	_____

21 LEISURELY QUESTIONS

GOAL

To identify facts about various leisure experiences.

FORMAT

Can be set up as a team or individual competition. The activity leader asks the 21 questions on the next two pages.

Teams or individuals rotate answering questions. After an answer, each other team (or individual) indicates whether the answer given was correct or incorrect. Scoring:

   2 points for a correct answer
   1 point for being accurate about the other team's or individual's answer

PROCESSING

Have participants reflect on how they/their team fared in the game.

MODIFICATION

As with all trivia games, frequent participants will learn the answers. An alternative is to have participants generate a question or two to share with the group. The leader can keep these questions for future games.

Leisurely Questions

1. MMA is associated with

Fighting*   Painting   Exploring

2. Starry Night's creator

Monet   Van Gogh*   Whistler

3. Center division of a backgammon board

Base   Bar*   Balance

4. Counts involved in a square dance "dos-a-dos"

Four   Six   Eight*

5. Different types of alcohol in a Long Island Iced Tea

Three   Five*   Seven

6. Nickname for the number 14 in Bingo

Double Lucky   Valentine's Day*   Two Touchdowns

7. Only species in all of the different brands of animal crackers

Horse   Lion   Elephant*

8. White glue is a key with this craft

Origami   Decoupage*   Stamping

9. Geocaching resembles this traditional activity

Capture the Flag   Treasure Hunt*   Kick the Can

10. Country that holds the record for most people singing karaoke at one time

Finland*   United States   Japan

11. A "gongoozler" is interested in

Geese   Canals*   Cheese

12. Height of the crossbar on a football goalpost

8'   10'*   12'

13. Most common letter in Scrabble

E*   A   R

14. Fictional city in the video games series Grand Theft Auto

Liberty*   Gotham   Freedom

15. Played the character Jeff Spicoli in "Fast Times at Ridgemont High"

Adam Sandler   Sean Penn*   Bill Murray

16. Location of the International Swimming Hall of Fame

Indianapolis*   San Diego   Fort Lauderdale

17. National League baseball team with the most world championships

Dodgers   Cardinals*   Pirates

18. Oldest one of these activities

Candyland*   Mr. Potato Head   Rubik's Cube

19. Where a docent volunteers

Hospital   Museum*   Church

20. Scooby Doo's nephew

Scrappy Doo*   Dandy Doo   Slappy Doo

21. Author of *Rabbit is Rich*

Vonnegut   Irving   Updike*

*Correct answer = ***

INTERVIEWS

GOAL

To share information and stimulate an individual's awareness of his or her own leisure lifestyle.

FORMAT

Participants divide into pairs, are given a pen and two index cards, and are instructed to interview each other in regards to leisure interests, hobbies, etc., writing answers down on card.

After 10 minutes or so, partners switch interviewer/interviewee positions and repeat the process.

Depending on the group, questions can be provided, participants can come up with their own questions, or a combination of the two. Sample questions might be:

- Where would you like to be on a summer afternoon?
- What do you like to do on a rainy day?
- If you could go anywhere in the world, where would you go?
- What new skill(s) would you like to learn?

PROCESSING

Have participants share what they found out and respond to some general questions.

- Was it difficult to come up with responses?
- Does your lifestyle lack regular leisure activity?
- Did partners learn anything from the interview and the information shared?

As we focus on the quality of work, so should we focus on improving the quality of our leisure experiences and incorporating these into our daily activities.

IDEAL DREAM VACATION

GOAL

To encourage a positive, creative, non-threatening attitude regarding leisure.

FORMAT

Take a vacation! You have no internal or external limitations.

Be specific and note dates, times, places, and people involved.

Remember — the sky's the limit! You are free to create, dream, and have fun!

PROCESSING

Ask participants to share their "dream vacation." Does the description include past experiences? Discuss the reality of following through with the activities described.

MODIFICATIONS

A vacation, especially a dream vacation, can take a long time, but the length of time is only one aspect of leisure experiences. Leisure can happen in shorter periods of time, too. Ask participants for their dream way to spend a free hour in the middle of the day or a free day when there are no responsibilities that need to be met.

LEISURE TIMELINE CONTINUUM

GOAL

To identify past activities and interests with the intent of identifying and exploring present and future leisure interests or possibilities.

FORMAT

This can be done with groups utilizing a large-scale timeline posted on the wall or using a sheet like the one on the next page for individuals.

Participants begin by identifying their earliest memories of leisure experiences and continue on up through their current age, as well as identifying future interests and dreams.

Encourage creative, artistic expression (e.g., drawing a boat instead of writing the word "sailing").

PROCESSING

This allows folks the opportunity to rely on themselves as a resource; we all have our own "leisure bank." Sometimes we just need the opportunity and freedom to tap into it.

- What is your earliest leisure memory?
- What did you do as a child?
- How have your leisure interests changed?
- Did any specific life event alter your leisure experiences?
- What would you like to try that you have never done before?
- What interests would you like to renew?

This is also a good activity for sharing information about selves and gaining insight into new interests/ideas.

Pictures of Leisure Experiences

Draw pictures that show experiences at these ages, or things you would like to experience when you reach these ages.

5

10

15

20

25

30

35

40

45

50

55

60

65

70

75

80

85

90

95

100

YOU MAKE THE CALL

GOAL

To identify activity preferences.

FORMAT

Use a large plain ball. Use a marker to divide the ball into sections and write a question appropriate to the group you're working with in each section. For example, with high school students:

- Favorite reality show?

- Favorite school subject?

- Shop on-line or at a mall?

- Worst job you ever had?

- Pizza or pasta, tacos, or hamburgers?

- Favorite candy?

Include a section called "Free Space."

Toss the ball to a participant. When they catch it, call out the name of a particular finger or thumb, for example, "right pinkie."

The participant must then answer the question in the space that their right pinkie is touching. If their finger is in the "Free Space," they can answer any of the questions on the ball.

After they answer, participants toss the ball to someone else and the process repeats until all have had a chance to respond.

PROCESSING

Have participants share something that they learned about someone else during the activity.

HAVE YOU EVER...

GOAL

To identify past leisure and life experiences.

FORMAT

Use a copy of the "Have You Ever" list on the next page or a similar list you've developed with items related to the background of your group.

Ask the group if they have ever done something that they were proud of but they didn't get any recognition for. Tell them that today they are going to be recognized for some past accomplishments.

Form a circle and instruct participants to step forward whenever they have done one of the accomplishments (from the "Have You Ever" list) that you share with them.

Group members who haven't done a particular item are instructed to clap and cheer for those who have.

PROCESSING

Have participants share something that's distinctive about their leisure that deserves recognition. It should be something they feel very few others would have done.

Have you ever...

- been bitten by a dog
- watched TV for 6 consecutive hours
- won a dance contest
- helped an animal give birth
- walked on stilts
- climbed a tree to rescue a cat
- kept a piece of chewed gum overnight and chewed it again
- seen a whale in the ocean
- survived a case of poison ivy
- drank 10 cups of coffee in a day
- taken a picture of your anatomy on a copy machine
- shot flies with a rubber band
- colored your hair orange, green, purple, or blue
- made ice cream by hand
- milked a cow or goat
- jumped off a bridge into water
- survived touching an electric fence
- won a game of Candyland
- been in a parade
- written a letter more than five pages long

SOME OF US...

GOAL

To identify commonalities in a group regarding activity and leisure experiences.

FORMAT

Have enough "bases" for each group member to have one. Begin with all participants (except you as the leader) standing in a circle on a base — only one person per base.

Explain that "I'm going to say something that is true about me. If the statement is also true about you, you'll need to leave the base you're on and move to another base. All the statements must have something to do with recreation and leisure."

Make your statement (e.g., some of us like country music, some of us have been to Alaska, some of us love to work out) and move to an open base.

The person who does not get a base becomes the new "it" and says something that's true about himself or herself beginning with the phrase "Some of us…"

PROCESSING

Have participants share a highlight or low point of the activity for them.

PICTURES

GOAL

To identify the progression of a leisure activity in your life.

FORMAT

Participants are asked to create "My Leisure Cartoon" which depicts the history of their involvement with a particular activity.

PROCESSING

Ask each participant to share the story depicted in his or her cartoon.

My Leisure Cartoon

PAY TO PLAY

GOAL

To recognize the relationship of leisure to money.

FORMAT

Participants work as teams in a "Price is Right" format to estimate the cost of various leisure activities or pieces of equipment.

Each team, in a rotating sequence, bids on the item and the team closest to the actual price (without going over the price) wins a point.

Each team could suggest an item or experience (and you could do a computer search to find the current best price), generic items can be used, or you can price specific experiences in your community. For example (The prices in parentheses were accurate when the book was published, but a search for up-to-date prices is something we suggest.):

- Game-Day Field Box Seat at Yankee Stadium ($300)

- Hannah Montana 2: Meet Miley Cyrus CD ($19.99)

- 6 Boxes (24 pack) of Crayola Washable Crayons ($19.85)

- Franklin Expert 115 mm Bocce Ball Set ($114.99)

- Regular Admission at Hershey (PA) Park ($52.95)

A final challenge for the group might be to select from a group of 10-12 items/experiences those three that could be purchased for under $100.

PROCESSING

Have participants follow up their consideration of leisure costs with a look at their personal expenditures by:

- Charting their leisure/recreation spending for a period of time.

- Estimating the monthly cost of their favorite activities or hobbies.

- Generating low- or no-cost alternatives to some of their activities or hobbies.

THE ROOM

GOAL

To identify personal leisure preferences and preferred environment.

FORMAT

Give each participant a blank sheet of paper and something to write with.

Their challenge is to create a 300-square-foot room that contains 10-15 objects. They will be staying in the room for a month.

PROCESSING

Have participants share their rooms, focusing on what they perceive to be the most critical features for enjoyment.

Recognition

You have to take life as it happens, but you should try to
make it happen the way you want to take it.

— Old German Saying

"Reflecting" entails gaining some personal insights regarding leisure. "Recognition" involves expanding the meaningfulness of these insights by exploring their relationships with other aspects of life. Specifically, how does leisure impact upon relationships, or work, or physical fitness, or sexuality, and how do all of these affect leisure? How, too, do participant's individual priorities and motivators square with their perceptions of leisure? Also, the matter of values. Do their deeds match their creeds?

THE COMPANY PICNIC

GOAL

To identify leisure preferences.

FORMAT

Participants are presented with the scenario on the following page. They are asked to answer the questions at the end of the scenario as a way to compare their choices of leisure in different social situations.

PROCESSING

Participants are asked to share their responses and to reflect on whether their answers:

- Match their lifestyles and choices they actually make.

- Would have been different had their spouse or friends been with them.

- Are what they ideally would want them to be.

The Company Picnic

You have just arrived at your spouse's company picnic. Your spouse remembers that s/he has forgotten something at home that s/he had promised to bring. S/he says, "Have fun, I'll be right back" and takes off to get whatever was forgotten.

You are left alone with a group of strangers. As you look around the scene, you observe eight distinct clusters of people involved in the activities below:

A. Sports people

volleyball and horseshoes

B. Artists

jam session and sing-a-long

C. Socializers

charades and other party games

D. Spectators

taking in the scene

E. Entrepreneurs

discussing investments and the economy

F. Naturalists

organizing a nature walk

G. Builders/Organizers

setting up tables and preparing food

H. Isolates

"hanging out"

Which do you join with? _____

After 15 minutes, the group breaks up. Which of the other groups do you join now?

_____

After a while this group too breaks up. Which of the remaining groups will you move to?

_____

WHAT'S KEEPING ME FROM HAVING FUN?

GOAL

To identify barriers to leisure fulfillment.

FORMAT

Using the set of statements on the next page, participants identify some of their barriers to leisure. Give each participant a copy of the statements and ask them to circle the most appropriate response to each statement.

PROCESSING

Have participants share the barrier that is toughest for them. Also, are any of the barriers connected?

WHAT'S KEEPING ME FROM HAVING FUN?

Look at the list below. Think of your present leisure lifestyle. Be honest in your reply.

Circle the number that reflects whether the statement is a barrier for you (1) Rarely, (2) Sometimes, or (3) Almost Always

R	S	AA	
1	(2)	3	1. I often don't feel like doing anything.
(1)	2	3	2. Too many family obligations.
1	(2)	3	3. Work is a main priority.
(1)	2	3	4. Caregiving takes up all my time.
(1)	2	3	5. I just don't think leisure is that important.
1	2	(3)	6. I really don't know what is meaningful right now.
1	(2)	3	7. Too much stress.
1	(2)	3	8. I am over-committed to too many things as it is.
1	(2)	3	9. Not enough money for leisure.
1	(2)	3	10. I don't have the skills needed.
1	(2)	3	11. I'm not artistic or creative.
1	(2)	3	12. I'm embarrassed to learn anything new.
(1)	2	3	13. I'm too old to learn anything new.
1	(2)	3	14. I don't have the time.
1	(2)	3	15. I don't know what is available.
1	(2)	3	16. I don't like learning new things.
1	2	(3)	17. I don't have anyone to go with.
(1)	2	3	18. I don't have anyone to take care of my care-receiver.
1	2	(3)	19. Social situations make me uncomfortable.
1	2	(3)	20. Making decisions is hard for me.
1	2	(3)	21. Following through on my decisions is difficult.
(1)	2	3	22. My health is not that good.
(1)	2	3	23. What good is leisure anyway?
1	(2)	3	24. Lack of transportation.
1	2	3	25. Any others not on this list? _____

46

IN THE FLOW

GOAL

To recognize the importance of the balance between personal skills and activity challenge levels.

FORMAT

Leader briefly explains the "flow" model shown on the next page and gives examples appropriate for the group. Basically the model shows that we are in the flow when our skill level matches the challenge of an activity. Too much challenge leads to frustration and too little challenge leads to boredom.

In a skiing example, appropriate levels of challenge (being in section "B" or "in the flow") occur, for example, when a skier of moderate ability takes on an intermediate slope. In "A" skills are lower than the required ability (e.g., a beginner on an intermediate hill) resulting in frustration and failure. In "C" it might be the opposite situation, intermediate skills on a novice hill. The result is boredom and rather quickly tiring of the activity.

Given this brief introduction to "flow," participants are then encouraged to consider activities they participate in. Have them place activities in the appropriate area of the model to show whether they are too difficult for current skill levels ("A"), too easy ("C"), or appropriately challenging ("B").

Have participants name the activities they need to "juice up" — to get into or back into the flow with key questions:

- What activities do you need a higher skill level in?
- What activities do you need a higher challenge level in?

Have participants also list activities where it might be appropriate to lower the challenge level to make the activity more satisfying.

PROCESSING

Participants share the activities they have listed and explain why they feel like they need to change their skills or challenge levels.

IN THE FLOW

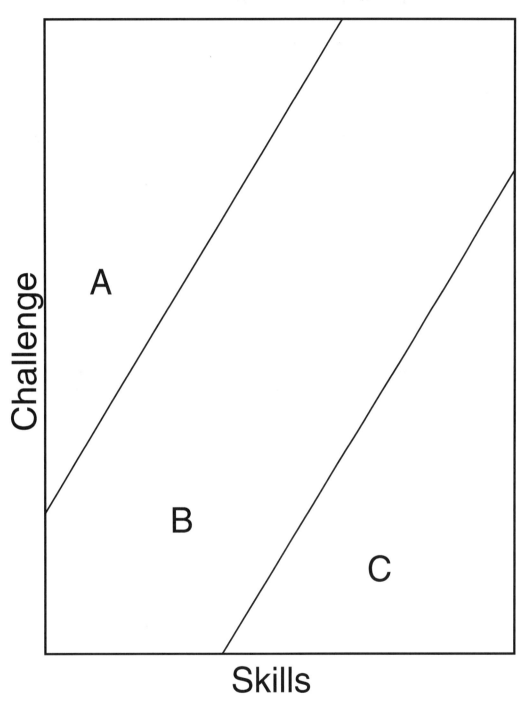

A. Too challenging

B. In the flow

C. Not challenging enough

THE BUMMER SCALE

GOAL

To identify how leisure activities might be utilized to mitigate life's setbacks.

FORMAT

The "Bummer Scale" shown on the next page is introduced with an appropriate story. As you read the story below, make sure the participants understand why the check marks were put where they were on the scale.

1. You're feeling great about a trip to the beach.

2. You jump into the car and really enjoy the scenery and the songs on the radio.

3. You're pulled over for speeding and given a ticket.

4a. You're so bummed out by the ticket that your day at the beach is ruined, or

4b. You go to the beach and have a good time.

Next, discuss or generate a list of "bummers" in the blank spaces of the Bummer Scale. It may help to classify them as minor, moderate, or major.

Given an understanding of what it is that "bugs" them, participants can next be encouraged to share ways in which leisure can assist with moving from the "frown" caused by bummers to the "smile" of no longer being down about them.

Discuss whether the participant's usual leisure activities are enough to remove the bummer. If not, what might need to be done?

PROCESSING

This exercise fits well into discussion of stress management. It also offers concrete examples of the re-creative or restorative powers of leisure. While leisure is typically discovered as valuable for coping with certain problems, its limits can also become evident.

For some groups the discussion may lead into whether using negative leisure choices, such as drugs and alcohol, really is effective at providing long-term relief from bummer situations.

A closing statement regarding the exercise: "Don't sweat the small stuff, almost everything is small stuff."

Bummer Scale

	😞	😊
1. trip to the beach		✓
2. enjoy the scenery and the songs		✓
3. pulled over for speeding and given a ticket	✓	
4a. day at the beach is ruined	✓	
4b. go to the beach and have a good time		✓

CAN'T GET THERE FROM HERE

GOAL

To recognize individuals affected by our lifestyles.

FORMAT

Read the scenario on the next page after explaining that this is an often-told story about a confused traveler that has much relevance to considering our lifestyles. It concerns a lost tourist and a native who have a conversation about the best way to go.

Next, participants are encouraged to identify individuals who do care about the direction of their lifestyles and to hypothesize regarding these individuals' aspirations for them.

Answer the questions:

- What do others expect of you?

- How would they react to changes you have in mind?

PROCESSING

As individuals share their perceptions of those affected by their leisure, several follow-up questions are often worth pursing:

- Can you think of compromises that might allow both your and their expectations to be met?

- How might leisure be utilized to strengthen relationships with these individuals?

Getting There

Tourist: (pulled off to the side of the road studying a road map) Do you know the way to Freeport?

Native: Yeah! (keeps on walking)

Tourist: No, wait, I mean will you help me with directions?

Native: Okay. (turns around and returns to car)

Tourist: According to the map it looks like there are two ways to get there.

Native: That's right. You could take High Road over there (points) or Frost Road back there. (points)

Tourist: Will it make any difference if I take High Road?

Native: Not to me it won't! (walks away)

The native does not have expectations for you!

- Who does have expectations for you?

- What do others expect of you?

- How would they react to changes you have in mind?

- Can you think of compromises that might allow both your and their expectations to be met?

- How might leisure be utilized to strengthen relationships with these individuals?

SIMON SAYS

GOAL

To identify personal barriers to fully realize leisure potentials.

FORMAT

Group participates in the old favorite "Simon Says" encouraged by the challenge of expressing their playfulness or of winning a prize if Simon can't stump them.

After as many preliminary moves as you like, the command "Simon says jump into the air" is followed immediately by "come down."

Everyone loses.

The question though, just as in the game, is whether there are there things that ground our best intentions for change in our lifestyles? What are these barriers? What can we do about them?

PROCESSING

A listing of barriers can be made with brainstorming or discussion of potential solutions.

Categories useful in organizing these barriers include personal skills, personal attitudes or motivation, resources (time, money, equipment), environment (where you live), and attitudes of others including opposing choices.

AMISH EVENING

GOAL

To identify personal level of dependency on technology.

FORMAT

Have participants consider what a typical evening of leisure consists of and how much of their leisure involves technology.

Next have them consider what a technology-free evening for them could consist of and what potentials such an evening would create.

PROCESSING

Have participants share their perspectives.

Follow up by developing a plan for a low-tech weekend.

An alternative is to share the following three words that are core Amish values: simplicity, community, and faithfulness.

Ask participants to give examples of how each could be demonstrated in a lifestyle.

ON MOTIVATION

GOAL

To recognize the relationship between personal motivators and leisure participation.

FORMAT

Participants are asked to use circles, triangles, squares, and S's in drawing a picture or making a design. Their drawings are then interpreted (by themselves) using the following key:

Circles = family motivation
Triangles = success
Squares = security
S = sex

Next, participants are asked how accurate this interpretation is for them. The point is made that it's difficult to generalize about motivation, but that experts (McClelland) have come up with some common denominators: affiliation, power, achievement, and love.

Explain each of the motivators.

- Affiliation (with others, with something beyond self)

- Power (over self/others)

- Achievement (realization of goals/objectives)

- Love (for people, things)

Participants are asked to relate their typical activities to various motivators as shown in the top four rows on the next page. Ask participants if the marks shown are true for them.

Have participants include more activities and rate them on the types of motivations proposed by McClelland.

PROCESSING

Participants then review the extent to which their activities rate in the various motivational characteristics and the extent to which each motivator is present in their activities.

McClelland's Motivators

Activity	Affiliation	Power	Achieve-ment	Love
Reading	-	+	O	O
Swimming	-	+	-	O
Gambling	+	O	O	+
TV	O	O	O	+

o = no relationship
- = negative relationship
+ = positive relationship

ON NEEDS

GOAL

To recognize the relationship between personal needs and leisure participation.

FORMAT

Participants complete the needs exercise on the next page. They are then asked to compare their list of needs with the activities that are most prevalent in their leisure.

PROCESSING

Have participants list their five most important needs in order of priority. Have them identify how they are meeting each one through leisure. How often? If having trouble doing so, why?

NOTE: The next activity, "Needs vs. Activities," provides another method for processing this information.

It Is Important For Me

Below is a list of need statements. Read the list carefully and then check off the 7 - 10 needs that are very important to you in your leisure. After selecting the top needs, go back and mark the most important need with a 1 and use 2 through 5 to indicate the others in your top five.

It is important for me to:

____ do something meaningful

____ be physically active

____ be committed to something

____ keep busy

____ do lots of different things

____ relax and take it easy

____ do something different from work/school

____ be entertained

____ be able to do what I want

____ experience new and novel things

____ be spontaneous

____ develop abiding friendships

____ be in attractive or natural surroundings

____ learn more about myself

____ compete with others

____ compete with myself to do better or overcome some challenge or risk

____ make and carry out plans

____ be a success at what I do

____ develop, improve, and make use of my skills

____ be creative

____ have something to show for my efforts

____ strengthen family togetherness

____ meet new people

____ get recognition and approval for what I do

____ have feelings of personal worth and confidence

____ laugh and enjoy and celebrate

____ help others

____ other _____

NEEDS vs. ACTIVITIES

GOAL

To recognize the relationship between personal needs and leisure activity participation.

FORMAT

After review of the needs in the "On Needs" exercise, participants are asked to determine the relationship between their three to five most common leisure activities and their three to five top priorities among needs. For example:

Needs Compared to Activities			
	TV Watching	Volleyball	Reading
Help Others	0	1	0
Strengthen Family Togetherness	1	1	1
Be Creative	0	1	1

Potential for meeting each need is rated from 0 = minimal through 3 very high.

PROCESSING

Focus can be on three major questions:

- Are there needs that your activities are not meeting?

- Are there specific activities that aren't meeting your needs?

- What activities might improve the level of need being met?

Needs Compared to Activities

Across the top, list your five most common activities. Down the left side, list your five most common needs. In the other boxes list the potential each activity has for meeting each need. If there is minimal potential, put a 0 in the box. Go up to 3 if there is a very high potential.

Activities ➜ Needs ⬇					

REPORT CARD

GOAL

To analyze the relationship between leisure and interpersonal skills.

FORMAT

Participants are asked to rate themselves on each of the characteristics shown on the score sheet — all of which they are first asked to define. There are three columns for ratings:

- self, how the participant thinks he or she rates on the characteristic

- others, how a spouse or boss might rate the participant

- ideal, how the participant would like to be rated

Following this, participants are asked to circle one or two of the characteristics in which they would most like to improve. In doing their "improve" choices, they are asked to relate how leisure experiences and activities might allow them opportunities to improve.

PROCESSING

In addition to utilizing the exercise as it is described above, the characteristics (cooperation, trust, etc.) can be monitored at subsequent sessions with comments sought on perceived improvement in identified areas of need.

REPORT CARD

Briefly define each of the characteristics listed on the score sheet. Then rate yourself on each of the characteristics. There are three columns for ratings:

- Self, how you think you rate on the characteristic
- Others, how a spouse or boss might rate you
- Ideal, how you would like to be rated

Use the following scale for you ratings:

5 = excellent

4 = very good

3 = good

2 = adequate

1 = poor

0 = pathetic

	Definition	**Self**	**Others**	**Ideal**
Cooperation				
Trust				
Leadership				
Sense of Humor				
Courage/ Risk-Taking				

GOING FOR THE BURN

GOAL

To recognize the relative caloric cost of various activities.

FORMAT

Working as an individual or as part of a team, participants are asked to rank the activities which follow from lowest = 1 to highest = 11 in regard to the number of calories which are burned as you participate.

PROCESSING

The correct order is 3, 9, 5, 2, 1, 6, 8, 11, 10, 4, 7. Discuss why various activities burn calories and clear up any misconceptions about the order participants came up with.

Have participants identify how they could burn additional calories by tweaking their typical day.

Calorie Burners

Each of the following activities burns a certain number of calories per hour. Rank the activities from the one that burns the fewest number of calories = 1 to the one that burns to most calories = 11.

___ Bowling

___ Elliptical Trainer

___ Golf (Walking and Pulling Cart)

___ Hatha Yoga

___ Ironing

___ Line Dancing

___ Skiing (Cross-country)

___ Step Aerobics

___ Swimming (moderate)

___ Table Tennis

___ Walking (4 mph)

PRECIOUS TIME

GOAL

To reflect on priorities for time use.

FORMAT

Working as an individual or with a partner, participants are asked to complete one of the following sentences:

1. Life is too short to _____.

                                        Or

2. Life is too short not to _____.

Play the song "Precious Time" by Van Morrison while participants come up with their responses.

PROCESSING

Have each pair or individual share what they have come up with.

LAUGH-THINK-CRY

GOAL

To identify the impact of leisure experiences.

FORMAT

Leader briefs group by relating that laughing, thinking, and crying were the three things the late Jim Valvano said people needed every day.

Next the group members say one of the three actions in rotation around the group (first person says laugh, second says think, and so on). The leader then asks people to come up with an example of something that usually makes them do the one of the three they have just said (e.g., watching little kids eat spaghetti always makes me laugh).

Finally participants group by the action they said and come up with 2-3 suggestions for getting themselves or their family/team/organization doing more of that action.

PROCESSING

To summarize the above, have participant groups share their plans for action.

PET PEEVES

GOAL

To identify aspects of leisure and recreation that are annoying.

FORMAT

Leader provides examples of general (e.g., slow drivers) and leisure/recreation (too many commercials on TV) pet peeves. Participants are then asked to come up with a pet peeve related to their leisure and recreation.

PROCESSING

Participants share their peeves as well as thoughts on how they could cope more effectively with them.

10 THINGS TO DO WITH "10 THINGS I LOVE TO DO"

GOAL

To analyze personal leisure patterns.

FORMAT

Asking participants in leisure education programs to list their five or ten or twenty most enjoyed experiences/activities is perhaps the single most utilized programming technique.

Typical analysis of these lists includes:

- amount of time experience takes
- number of times you've done the experience in the last one to six months
- cost of experience
- number of people you usually have involved with the experience
- whether you typically supplement the experience with alcohol or drugs
- whether it requires equipment
- whether it requires risk
- whether you can do it spontaneously
- whether or not you still anticipate being involved with the experience at age 65
- whether the activity takes place indoors or out

Have participants make a list of their ten favorite activities or experiences on the following score sheet. Select one or more of the topics listed above and ask participants to analyze their list relative to that topic.

PROCESSING

Go through the participants' analysis, looking at ways to increase the ability to do leisure activities or remove barriers.

In addition to the above, ask participants to identify five things they would like to try. Use the same kind of analysis as described above for these activities.

10 Things I Love to Do

List your 10 favorite leisure activities or leisure experiences. Analyze them based on the question the group leader asks. In your answer include whether the topic being discussed makes it more or less likely you will participate in the activity.

Activity	Analysis

FEELINGS

GOAL

To identify the feelings associated with various leisure activities.

FORMAT

Leader prepares slips with brief descriptions of leisure experiences. For example:

- singing in a choir
- watching a baseball game on TV
- listening to a CD by your favorite artist
- doing a crossword puzzle
- eating ice cream
- chatting with friends on Facebook
- petting an energetic puppy
- SCUBA diving
- camping in the wilderness
- running a marathon

Participants draw a slip, read it to the group, and state the feeling it generates.

PROCESSING

Have participants share their responses. One approach is to have one person give his or her answer. Then ask who had an identical or similar response and who had something very different.

Rather than generic experiences, you may want to have participants generate a list of common experiences in their community. You can also use the experiences listed in the previous exercise, 10 Things I Love to Do.

WOULD YOU RATHER HAVE?

GOAL

To identify personal values and goals.

FORMAT

Participants complete the Preferences exercise on the next page. With each of the four sets of possibilities they are asked to rank their interest in each from 5 (top pick) to 1 (last pick).

When they are through with ranking each set, have the participants total up their preferences by adding all the scores for choice A together, all the scores for choice B, and so on.

The meaning of each set is as follows:

A = wealth

B = the body

C = recognition

D = the mind

E = relationships

PROCESSING

Have participants identify their top value and recognize others in the group who share it.

Preferences

With each of the four sets of possibilities, rank your interest from 5 (top pick) to 1 (last pick).

When you are through ranking each set, total up your preferences by adding all the scores for choice A together, all the scores for choice B, and so on in the spaces below.

Set 1

_____ A. $1,000 a week for life

_____ B. incredibly good looks

_____ C. a literary prize for your writing

_____ D. incredibly strong faith

_____ E. a loving spouse/partner

Set 2

_____ A. impressive stock portfolio

_____ B. impressive strength and build

_____ C. impressive article about you in *People* magazine

_____ D. impressive confidence and self-esteem

_____ E. impressive number of friends

Set 3

_____ A. lottery jackpot of $250,000

_____ B. professional level athletic skills

_____ C. a scientific award for your research

_____ D. a phenomenal level of community service

_____ E. co-workers who support and admire you

Set 4

_____ A. you own your dream house and car

_____ B. your health and fitness are exemplary

_____ C. you're elected to political office

_____ D. you're a valued member of your religious group

_____ E. your family is close and caring

Totals: A ___ B ___ C ___ D ___ E ___

LEISURE SWAP

GOAL

To share information about a personal leisure interest and recognize the interests of others.

FORMAT

Participants are asked to prepare a 5-10 minute "Show and Tell" of one of their favorite leisure activities. They are encouraged to demonstrate the equipment (e.g., a GPS system for geocaching) or the techniques (e.g., tying a fly with fishing) associated with their activity.

PROCESSING

Have participants share which of the activities they learned about will be considered in their future plans.

CRUISING

GOAL

To reflect on personal values/priorities for leisure.

FORMAT

Tell participants to pretend they are taking a cruise. Have them review the list on the next page that shows the 20 activities that are available and select their top five.

PROCESSING

Have participants share their choices and summarize them with a word or phrase that would reflect their "philosophy of taking a cruise."

Cruise Events

Pretend you are onboard a cruise ship. Review the list of 20 activities available today and select your top five.

1. Learning Spanish

2. Spinning

3. Swing Dancing

4. Scrapbooking

5. Watercolor Class

6. Jameson Whiskey Tasting

7. Karaoke

8. Texas Hold'em Tournament

9. Tai Chi

10. Golf Putting Tournament

11. Wii Guitar Hero

12. Photoshop Class

13. How To Boost Your Metabolism

14. Trivia Contest

15. Faberge Showcase

16. Yoga

17. Salsa Dancing

18. Rock and Roll Party

19. Fast Cash Bingo

20. Secrets to a Flatter Stomach

L.I.F.E. (Leisure Is Fabulously Exciting)

GOAL

To identify potential outcomes of participation in leisure and recreation experiences and activities.

FORMAT

Participants are given examples of several acronyms that highlight potential outcomes of participating in leisure/recreation activities (e.g., L.I.F.E., as above). Included are activities (e.g., P.I.E, Photography Is Exciting) and terms/concepts (e.g., P.E.S.T., Play Eliminates Stressful Thoughts). They are encouraged to generate one of their own related to leisure and recreation.

PROCESSING

Have participants share their acronyms. Additionally have them generate an acronym for the leisure education program/group (e.g., C.A.L.F., Considering Alternatives for Leisure and Fun!)

LIFESTYLE COACHES

GOAL

To identify personal role models for various lifestyle components.

FORMAT

Share the following categories with participants:

- Adventure/excitement

- Appearance/looks

- Artistic expression

- Finances/investments

- Health/fitness

- Intelligence/wisdom

- Power/leadership

- Service/caring

- Social/fun

- Spiritual/religious

Tell participants that they can choose one of the areas and receive a "coach" to improve their performance/status in that area. Their choice should be a famous person associated with the area (e.g., Donald Trump for finances).

Next have them select a different category and, with this one, a coach from among people they know (e.g., cousin Fred for service). With this one they should add a comment on why they made the choice, because others may not know the individual (e.g., Fred is a long-time volunteer for the library).

PROCESSING

Have participants share their responses.

Additionally have them consider who within their group (or at the facility they're at) would be a good choice for coaching each of the 10 characteristics. See if participants have a way to ask for coaching from the people they named.

Lifestyle Coaches

Choose the lifestyle area below that you would most like to improve and then pick a "coach" to improve your performance/status in that area. Your choice should be a famous person associated with the area (e.g., Donald Trump for finances).

Next select a different category and, with this one, a personal coach from among people you know (e.g., cousin Fred for service). With this one add a comment on why you made the choice because others may not know the individual (e.g., Fred is a long-time volunteer for the library).

If you want to, you can add coaches in all of the ten areas you are interested in improving.

Lifestyle Area	Famous coach	Personal coach	Reason why
Adventure/excitement			
Appearance/looks			
Artistic expression			
Finances/investments			
Health/fitness			
Intelligence/wisdom			
Power/leadership			
Service/caring			
Social/fun			
Spiritual/religious			

I SEE FROM WHERE I STAND

GOAL

To identify influences on personal lifestyle, leisure values, and activities.

FORMAT

Begin with the statement that the Haitian proverb "I see from where I stand" is important to remember in thinking about lifestyle decisions. Individuals have diverse experiences in their lives, and this diversity is reflected in the diverse perspectives they bring to perceptions of what "the good life" or the "optimal lifestyle" might be. Encourage participants to cite a memorable experience and a message from each of the following potential influences:

1. The people who raised them

2. Siblings and friends

3. Community organizations, including church, school, and groups

4. The media

PROCESSING

Have participants share their memorable moments and messages and perhaps identify a role model (or someone they wouldn't want to model) from their past in regard to leisure.

FAITH MATTERS OR MATTERS OF FAITH

GOAL

To identify the impact of faith on personal leisure, lifestyle values, and attitudes.

FORMAT

List the following areas and encourage participants to consider the influence of each on their lifestyle/leisure choices.

1. Religious services and sponsored activities (what you participate in and how often).

2. Attitudes about your physical being (what your faith tells you about fitness, appearance, sexuality, and so forth).

3. Attitudes about your social being (what your faith tells you about family, relationships, friendships, working with others, and so forth).

4. Attitudes about your spiritual and emotional being (what your faith tells you about connecting to a higher power, finding joy and contentment, understanding your purpose and mission, serving others).

5. Relationship of faith to the decisions you make about leisure and lifestyle (what faith leads you toward and away from).

6. Relationship of faith to certain emotions (how faith influences the frequency and intensity of any of the following for you: love, passion, guilt, joy, peace, competitiveness, anger, or confusion).

PROCESSING

Encourage participants to share one or two insights from their review of the faith-related questions. Pose the question "What's the biggest impact of faith on your leisure?" as a wrap-up question.

Reaffirmation

And there were three men
Went down the road
As down the road went he,
The man they saw, the man he was
And the man he wanted to be.

— John Masefield

We all have many things that we would like to become. Like the restaurant menu, though, we can't realistically devour it all. In saying reaffirmation rather than simply affirmation, we are acknowledging that participants typically are, in stating goals for the future, returning to previously held beliefs or ideals — beliefs and ideals that have been suppressed, forgotten, perhaps even rejected for a period of time.

Their resurfacing often reflects a new appreciation for the payoffs they offer. These payoffs, it can be hoped, afford the opportunity for real personal needs, rather than only temporal wants to be satisfied. Ideally too, they speak to a life well lived, a life fully lived in which the ideal and the real often mesh.

The act of renewal (be it a magazine subscription or our wedding vows) indicates that we have realized the value of something and want to make a commitment to its future. Reaffirmation implies repetition and persistence. The promises we make to ourselves and to others are seldom a once and done proposition.

LOOKING AHEAD

GOAL

To determine personal ideals and hopes for the future.

FORMAT

Give participants the survey on the next page and ask them to answer the questions.

Then have them imagine a future point in time (e.g., six months from now, a year, five years, during retirement) and briefly relate an ideal lifestyle at that time — what you'll be doing for work and play, relationships you'll have, etc. Tell them to keep the answers to the survey questions in mind as they contemplate this ideal future.

PROCESSING

Allow participants to share their scenarios, encouraging questions from others designed to clarify what their priorities for the future are.

Self-Survey

Answer the following questions about how you feel about your present life.

1. What could I still do that, if I don't, I'll most regret?

2. What have I finally begun to accept about my life?

3. What still makes me laugh?

4. What still makes me furious?

5. What do I no longer worry about?

6. What do I feel shackled to?

7. What is the unfinished business of my life?

8. What group would I really like to become a part of?

9. What four words describe me most?

10. What about myself do I most dislike?

Now imagine a future time (at least six months from now) and briefly relate an ideal lifestyle at that time — what you'll be doing for work and play, relationships you'll have, etc. Keep your answers to the questions above in mind as you contemplate this ideal future.

COULDA SHOULDA WOULDA

GOAL

To determine personal strategies for decision-making and critique their effectiveness.

FORMAT

Participants are asked to consider several of the major decisions regarding leisure and lifestyle they have made in their lives. Emphasis is placed on the method of making the decision rather than simply upon the choice made. Questions to trigger discussion include:

- How did you decide?

- Who helped?

- Did you weigh the alternatives?

- How do you make decisions?

- Could you be more effective? And, if so, how?

PROCESSING

Depending upon the group, this exercise might be enhanced by presenting a "decision tree" concerning one of the participant's situations.

For example:

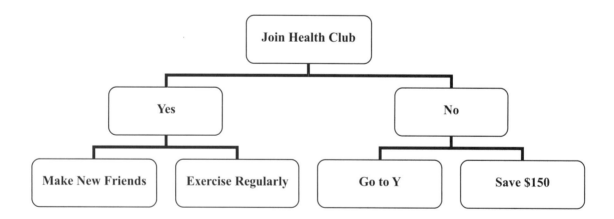

G.A.S.

GOAL

To demonstrate an understanding of Goal Attainment Scaling (G.A.S.).

FORMAT

The principle of the goal attainment scaling is introduced through an example:

"I want to lose weight. I would be disappointed if after a week of trying, my weight actually went up. If it at least stayed the same, I would feel ok. If I lost a few pounds, I'd be happy. I'd be ecstatic if it were more than five pounds."

Next, participants are asked to develop a continuum of outcomes, similar to that above, for a leisure goal of theirs.

PROCESSING

Developing a G.A.S. continuum fits well with presenting the concept of multiple outcomes or payoffs for participation in an activity. The "all eggs in one basket" approach of expecting and accepting only one type of reward for participation might too often cause individuals to give up on an activity that is doing a lot for them.

LEISURE INDEX: RECREATION ROLODEX

GOAL

To recognize resources for leisure awareness and participation.

FORMAT

Participants are asked to identify places and people and information sources useful in each of the following categories:

- Finding out what's happening or available

- Participating with you — activity and person(s)

- Activity file — things to do and where to do them

PROCESSING

Participants share ideas and add resources they've gleaned from others that may be of interest (e.g., phone number for "alcohol-free" events line, listings of Community Education/Recreation Departments).

BOXES

GOAL

To determine and prioritize ruts or boxes in personal lifestyles which need to be changed.

FORMAT

Participants are challenged with the following puzzle:

Placing your pencil on any of the corner dots, without raising your pencil off the page or tracing back over your lines, make four straight lines that intersect with all the dots.

Answer:

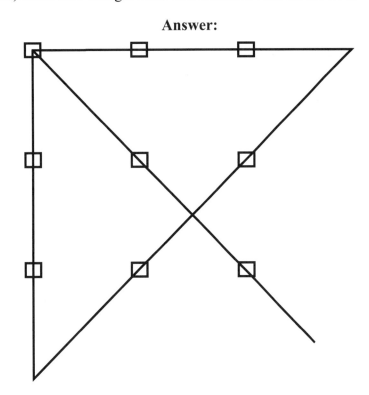

PROCESSING

The puzzle requires that we look beyond the box to solve it. In regard to leisure and lifestyle, in what areas do you most wish to expand beyond your current box or rut? What problems (puzzles) might such expansion allow you to solve?

Another variation in follow-up is to review the "Boxes of Life" suggested by Richard Bolles — learning, working, playing, and how they can be integrated into each day, week, month, and year rather than segmented as we traditionally do.

A third variation is to begin problem-solving on the puzzle with the challenge of doing it with five lines (very easy to do), then to try again with four (difficult), and then finally with three (impossible), making the point that to mean something our goals in leisure, like our leisure, need to be in the "flow" — challenging enough to give us a sense of accomplishment in achieving them, but not so difficult as to cause us to give up on goal setting altogether.

Boxes Puzzle

Place your pencil on any of the corner dots, without raising your pencil off the page or tracing back over your lines, make four straight lines that intersect with all the dots. You may cross your lines.

□   □   □

□   □   □

□   □   □

A POTPOURRI OF GOALS

GOAL

To determine how diverse personal leisure goals might be integrated through various leisure experiences/activities.

FORMAT

Participants review the goals on the following page, checking those that they feel apply to them.

Reponses are shared.

Then participants are challenged to think of an activity/experience that would allow for the realization of several of the goals they have chosen.

PROCESSING

Participants are encouraged to share goals and activities to meet them. Feedback from other participants is encouraged particularly in regard to additional ideas for "goal-meeting" activities.

Goals Galore

Check the goals in the lists below that apply to you.

LEISURE GOALS

☐ To value my free time

☐ To know what's available for leisure

☐ To find more time for leisure

☐ To recognize low and no-cost leisure alternatives

☐ To find people to enjoy leisure with

☐ To feel motivated for leisure

☐ To feel less guilty about "playing"

☐ To be less restricted by family, spouse, or friends

☐ To eliminate barriers (e.g., transportation, insufficient funds), to my leisure

INTEREST GOALS

☐ To build on an old interest/skill

☐ To learn a new hobby/skill

☐ To be more spontaneous/humorous

☐ To be more involved in community functions

☐ To get more education

☐ To get more assertive

☐ To get more organized

☐ To study self-improvement/meditation

PHYSICAL GOALS

☐ To improve my fitness level/stamina

☐ To get outdoors more

☐ To slow down/relax

☐ To develop sport/game skills

☐ To be more active

☐ To reduce feelings of stress

SOCIAL GOALS

☐ To strengthen old friendships

☐ To build new friendships

☐ To strengthen family togetherness

☐ To do more things on my own

☐ To get involved with a group

List an activity or experience that allows you to meet several of the goals you checked.

LOW AND NO-COST

GOAL

To recognize low or no-cost community alternatives for leisure and determine how they relate to projected "new" lifestyles.

FORMAT

Participants review a list of "low and no-cost alternatives" shown on the next page and indicate how much use of each they make.

The response sheet also has a place for listing the programs that are available at each alternative. Ask participants to list programs they might be interested in, or make a list of all the programs that are available.

PROCESSING

Go through how well participants are using low and no-cost alternatives.

Beyond the question of how much they're using them, participants might consider if, in fact, they know what the places have to offer. For example, ask the group to discuss what they think the recreation department in their town offers and have them compare their responses with a program bulletin from the department.

Low and No-Cost

Review this list of low and no-cost recreation alternatives shown in the first column. In the second column indicate how much use you make of each of them. In the third column, list some of the programs that are available.

Resource	What you do there now	What kind of programs are available
YMCA, YWCA		
Churches		
Town or city recreation department		
Libraries		
State and local parks		
Service clubs		
Volunteer service opportunities		

CONTRACT

GOAL

To affirm or reaffirm a commitment to a changed lifestyle and to specify how the change will occur.

FORMAT

Have the participants fill out the contract for a Leisure Action Plan on the next page.

PROCESSING

Encourage individuals to share their plans utilizing "I will" statements as well as "because" explanations. For example, "Within three months I will be a member of the local Y, because it's an opportunity to be more fit and to make new friends."

NOTE

Another version of the contract is included in the next activity

Leisure Action Plan

Fill out the Leisure Action Plan as a way to keep track of your successes in changing your leisure.

Goals		
Steps toward Achieving	Immediately after discharge	
	Within three months	
	Within six months	
	Within a year	
Payoffs and Resources for Achievement		
My Leisure Network of Support		

NO-DISCOUNT CONTRACT

GOAL

To affirm or reaffirm a commitment to a changed lifestyle and to specify how the change will occur.

FORMAT

Have the participants fill out the No-Discount Contract on the next page.

PROCESSING

Begin with the thought that successful sales people have been known to post a picture in their work area of something they would love to have (boat, car, etc.). The picture serves as a motivator.

Have participants focus on #4 (benefits) and describe what the picture of their success would look like.

No-Discount Contract

Fill out this contract for each need you want to meet.

Contract

I, _____, have a right to get the following need met, and I agree to involve myself, and to be active to meet my need.

1. List your need.

I, _____, want to _____

_____

_____

_____

2. Make a list of requirements. Include all the things you have to do to go about getting this need met and all possibilities, no matter how far-fetched they may seem.

I, _____, will _____

_____

_____

_____

3. Figure out resources. Think of the people (spouse, children, mother/father, teacher, librarian, etc.) and the places you might need to go for help.

_____

_____

_____

_____

4. List the benefits. What will this do for you? Take a look at what you will have accomplished and give yourself credit for it.

When I succeed, I will _____

_____

_____

_____

_____

_____

ON SEIZING THE MOMENT

GOAL

To stimulate awareness of the approach individuals take to "time" in their lives.

FORMAT

Give the poem on the next page to individuals or share in a group, asking participant(s) to read out loud.

PROCESSING

Discuss attitudes towards life and allow each individual an opportunity to reaffirm what is important to him/her, and how we each have the opportunity to make the most of life now, so later on we don't look back and say, "I wish I had…"

I'd Pick More Daisies

If I had my life to live over,

> I'd try to make more mistakes next time.
>
> I would relax. I would limber up.
>
> I would be sillier than I have on this trip.
>
> I would be crazier. I would be less hygienic.
>
> I would take more chances, I would take more trips.
>
> I would climb more mountains, swim more rivers, and watch more sunsets.
>
> I would burn more gasoline. I would eat more ice cream and less beans.
>
> I would have more actual troubles and fewer imaginary ones.

You see, I am one of those people who lives prophylactically and sensibly and sanely, hour after hour, day after day.

Oh, I have had my moments

And if I had it to do over again, I'd have more of them.

In fact, I'd try to have nothing else.

> Just moments, one after another,
>
> Instead of living so many years ahead each day.

I have been one of those people who never go anywhere without a thermometer, a hot water bottle, a gargle, a raincoat, and a parachute.

If I had to do it over again, I would go places and do things.

> I'd travel lighter than I have.
>
> If I had my life to live over, I would start barefooted
>
> Earlier in the spring and stay that way later in the fall.
>
> I would play hooky more. I wouldn't make such good grades except by accident.
>
> I would ride on merry-go-rounds.

I'd pick more daisies!

Nadine Stair, age 85

MAGIC WAND

GOAL

To identify an ideal leisure scenario and perceived barriers to leisure pursuits and then determine steps to overcoming them.

FORMAT

1. Facilitator asks participant to identify REAL situation regarding a leisure dilemma or problem and list it on the From Real to Ideal form. For example, "I would love to visit my family but I don't have the time." Facilitator or participant notes the answer under REAL on scale.

2. Facilitator asks, "In reference to your IDEAL situation regarding [state leisure situation], if you had a magic wand, what would you wish?"

3. Participant responds, "If I had a magic wand, [describes IDEAL behavior or situation]."

4. Facilitator or participant notes answer under IDEAL on scale.

5. Facilitator then asks, "What would it take to get you from the REAL to the IDEAL regarding your problem area?"

6. Participant should list "barriers" to reaching the IDEAL. Put one in each space.

7. Facilitator should then guide the participant in addressing how to overcome each barrier until each has been eliminated on the way to the IDEAL situation.

PROCESSING

Have participants consider and share the personal characteristics (e.g., patience, assertiveness) most important in overcoming barriers.

From Real to Ideal

REAL	
Barrier	
Barrier	
Barrier	
Barrier	
Barrier	
IDEAL	

1. Identify a REAL situation regarding a leisure dilemma or problem you have and list it in the box next to the word REAL.

2. If you could wave a magic wand, what would be the IDEAL situation regarding what you wrote in the REAL box? Put that in the box next to IDEAL.

3. Now list the "barriers" that are keeping you from reaching the IDEAL. Put one in each space.

4. If you have an idea how to overcome the barrier, make a note of your plan in the same box as the barrier.

CIRCLE TALK

GOAL

To verbalize plans and concerns about future leisure participation.

FORMAT

Prepare questions you would like your group to discuss. For example:

- What's #1 on your bucket list?

- What do you want to spend more time doing?

- Who needs you to be part of their leisure?

Have group members pair off then form two circles (one circle inside another circle) facing their partner.

Read the first question and have each person respond to it for one minute.

Have one of the circles rotate three people to the right or left and, with their new partner, give their opinions on the second question.

Repeat the procedure for the remaining questions.

PROCESSING

Have participants generate a question for a subsequent use of the activity. Select some of their responses and repeat the activity at another time.

DID PICASSO HAVE THE RIGHT IDEA?

GOAL

To identify personal perspectives on planfulness vs. spontaneity in leisure.

FORMAT

Leader shares the following thought from Pablo Picasso:

"If you know exactly what you are going to do, what is the point of doing it?"

PROCESSING

Participants are asked to share:

- Experiences where planning works best

- Experiences where spontaneity works best

Which of the two styles do they lean toward and how that's working out for them?

An alternative is to list a series of activities and have participants respond to whether spontaneity or determining an exact plan of action works best for them. Examples:

- A bike ride

- A religious service

- A vacation

- A fitness session

- A round of golf

- A garden

- A party

HURRY UP!

GOAL

To recognize personal time commitments and generate a plan for greater effectiveness.

FORMAT

Provide some background regarding hurried lifestyles. For example: Whether it's "living in the fast lane," "time deepening," or "multi-tasking," many people try to put too much into too little time. The result can be less than optimal performance and lower satisfaction with activities jammed into too tight of a timeline.

Next have participants identify:

- What parts of your average day and week are too crowded?

- How can you rearrange or restructure things to create less need to be doing too much at a time?

PROCESSING

Have participants consider the juggling analogy of having too many balls in the air. Are there some you can do away with?

Prioritize your current commitments and choose one or two that you could let go of. What would they be and how much time and stress would be saved by letting go of them?

THE TREE

GOAL

To recognize the relationship between values, activities, and outcomes.

FORMAT

Have participants complete "The Tree" identifying their personal values, activities, and outcomes.

PROCESSING

Have each participant give an example of how a value translates to a particular activity that creates a specific outcome.

The Tree

1. In each circle, write one Core Value (what's important to you in life).

2. In the boxes, list activities that you can engage in that will support your values or what you think is important in life.

3. In the fruit, identify benefits you receive from engaging in the activities you listed.

WELLNESS PERSPECTIVES

GOAL

To recognize personal strengths and weaknesses among components of wellness.

FORMAT

Have participants complete the "Components of Wellness Scale" rating their level of agreement with a variety of statements.

PROCESSING

Have participants share the area they scored highest and lowest in and identify an action which might improve their low score(s).

Components of Well-Being Scale

Use the following scale to indicate your level of agreement with the statements below:

0 = strongly disagree   1 = mildly disagree   2= unsure   3 = mildly agree   4 = strongly agree

_____ A. I relate well to others.

_____ B. I live my life hopefully.

_____ C. I live my life in conflict with my values and beliefs.

_____ D. I have poor health.

_____ E. I think in a focused way.

_____ F. I belong to social groups that I value.

_____ G. I learn eagerly.

_____ H. I feel controlled by others.

_____ I. I feel happy.

_____ J. I am optimistic.

_____ K. My leisure experiences positively impact other areas of my life.

_____ L. I have trouble solving problems.

_____ M. I have lots of energy.

_____ N. I have a sense of meaning and purpose.

_____ O. My fitness level is high.

_____ P. I find enjoyment in my leisure experiences.

_____ Q. I don't often get to do what I enjoy in my leisure.

_____ R. I don't have friends.

Scoring

Leisure:

K + P = ___ - Q = ___

Cognitive:

E + G = ___ - L = ___

Physical:

M + O = ___ - D = ___

Spiritual:

B + N = ___ - C = ___

Social:

A + F = ___ - R = ___

Psychological/Emotional:

I + J = ___ - H = ___

ACCORDING TO SARAH PALIN

GOAL

To determine prospective personal lifestyle changes.

FORMAT

Share the following thought, which Sarah Palin stated in an August 2010 interview with Chris Wallace:

"Only dead fish go with the flow."

Have participants relate the statement to their lifestyles, identifying two to three areas in which they go with the flow (what most people do) and two to three areas in which what they do is different from most folks.

PROCESSING

Have participants identify the pluses and the minuses of going with and going against the flow.

Finally, have each person identify one area where a switch in his or her pattern would be good for him or her.

ATTITUDES

GOAL

To identify personal attitudes that are barriers to leisure.

FORMAT

Briefly describe the following three categories of barriers to participation in various experiences:

- **Can't do:** don't know how, need to learn the skills (e.g., I can't swim!)

- **Won't do:** values or perceptions make it something to avoid (e.g., It's against my religious beliefs! Or, Men don't dance!)

- **Don't do:** time, financial, or other constraints (e.g., I've got too much work to do!)

Next encourage participants to identify a specific example of how each of these categories affects them.

PROCESSING

Have participants share examples and decide on one that they would like to change. Briefly outline what steps would be necessary to convert the *can't*, *won't* or *don't* into a *do*.

Social Skills

No one can make you feel inferior without your consent.

— Eleanor Roosevelt

Perceived and actual deficits in social confidence and competence often surface as a barrier to leisure participation and enjoyment. The exercises that follow are designed to offer practice in a variety of social skills. "A Potpourri of Social Needs" can provide individual group members with social goals while at the same time providing group leaders with a feel for group priorities. "Introduction Interviews" involves many skills and allows group members to "break the ice" with one another in a structured way. "Meetings and Greetings" focuses on difficulties specific to "breaking the ice" or initiating conversation in a new situation.

The lotto-like activities — "20 Questions," "Emotional Lotto," "Some of Us Have," "Dreams and Schemes," and "Some Unique People" all expand upon working with only one other group member. Each requires mingling with other group members. "Survey" extends the mingling and interaction beyond the group.

"And The Winners Are" is typical of cooperative group tasks useful in moving beyond conversation to working together. Old favorites such as Password or Jeopardy are useful in this regard as well. Additionally, trust activities, initiative problems, or cooperative challenges such as '"View-er, Clue-er, Do-er" or "A-Z" can provide opportunities in this regard. "Roles in Groups" and the "Cooperation and Trust Scale" can be used in conjunction with these activities.

Giving and receiving feedback is an important skill both in an affective sense, as the encouragement in "Positive Assertions" shows, and in a cognitive sense, as in "The Right Stuff."

Throughout the process of developing social skills through group involvement, a variety of icebreakers or introductory activities can be useful. On a basic level this might include stating one's name and goal for the group. Alternatives include sharing one's energy level, social ideal (person whose social skills you wish to model), social highlights from the past, or responding to a short exercise like the "Feelings Menu," "Continuum," or "Who Said It?"

Several general principles to consider in conducting social-skills training are

1. Model What You Preach — Both in the way you facilitate group sessions and in your contacts with group members beyond the group, it is vital to model good social skills. Greet people, break the ice, remember previous conversations, be an active listener, demonstrate empathy; in short, be and demonstrate the possibility of being the things that group members are identifying as goals.

2. Practice, Don't Just Preach — Provide opportunities within group sessions for some "real" practice of social skills. Have a party with group members serving as hosts, begin a group with an informal rap session, work as a group on a cooking or crafts project. Beyond the group sessions, assist group members in identifying the variety of social possibilities in their living environment. Challenge them to take advantage of some of these and to use the social skills group as a place to process their thoughts and feelings about these new experiences.

3. Provide and Encourage Feedback — Be consistent in responding to noted concerns and to progress toward or digressions from stated objectives. Show respect for the learned experience and opinions of group members but encourage other group members (and remember yourself) to be assertive in discussing alternatives to these opinions. Make a conscious effort to identify payoffs of enhanced social activity. Keep in mind that the ability to compromise is vital to social competence. Specific tips in this regard:

   • Recognize seemingly preoccupied or distressed group members with a comment such as "you seem to be having a difficult time today" and ask how the group might be of assistance.

   • Focus upon multiple potential benefits of enhanced social participation, avoiding the inevitable disappointment for group members who focus on only one expected payoff.

   • Cite discrepancies between verbalizations regarding social characteristics (e.g., "I can't maintain a conversation") and actual observed performance (e.g., "You and Tom seemed to really get into that interview. You talked for quite a while").

The RULE acronym for motivational interviewing (Rollnick, Miller, & Butler, 2008) provides a frame of reference for effective facilitation of change. Components include:

• <u>Resist</u> the righting reflex: Health care professionals have the tendency to fix things, prevent harm, etc. Humans have a natural tendency to resist persuasion. This approach by the health care provider to the client to prescribe or persuade often leads to resistance on the part of the client, especially when it involves behavior change.

• <u>Understand</u> and explore the client's own motivations: Assist the clients to identify their own reasons for change, as it is most likely to trigger behavior change (internal).

• <u>Listen</u> with empathy: This implies that the health care professional listens at least as much as s/he informs. The answers lie within the client, and the role of the health care professional is to facilitate this discovery.

• <u>Empower</u> the client: The client takes an active role of exploring so s/he can make a difference in his/her own health. This discovery assists the client in understanding s/he has the ability and resources to make this and other health behavior changes.

A POTPOURRI OF SOCIAL NEEDS

GOAL

To prioritize personal social needs and identify actions toward better meeting them.

FORMAT

Participants complete the Potpourri of Social Needs checklist either individually or (for the action section) with a partner with the same needs. It may be helpful to provide an example of a potential activity specific to a particular need (e.g., for strengthen family togetherness, how about a weekly games night).

PROCESSING

When participants have completed the checklist and actions, move through the list having participants share their prospective actions for each of the needs.

Potpourri of Social Needs

Review the following list placing a checkmark next to those statements that are true for you.

I need to:

_____ 1. Strengthen old friendships.

_____ 2. Build new friendships.

_____ 3. Strengthen family togetherness.

_____ 4. Get involved with a group/organization/club.

_____ 5. Be more involved with community functions.

_____ 6. Manage my time better.

_____ 7. Eliminate barriers (e.g., transportation, opposition by others).

_____ 8. Be more spontaneous.

_____ 9. Be more humorous.

_____ 10. Have regular opportunities to help others.

_____ 11. Enhance my conversational skills.

_____ 12. Enhance my social life at work and with co-workers.

_____ 13. Reduce my level of apprehension regarding meeting new people and facing new social situations.

_____ 14. Initiate discussion in group (express feelings/opinions).

_____ 15. Do more "fun" things.

_____ 16. Have a stronger network of people I can count on.

_____ 17. Improve listening skills.

_____ 18. Other _____

Now review those items above which you've checked and determine your top 3-5 priorities. List the numbers of these items in the spaces below:

_____   _____   _____   _____   _____

Finally, list some actions/activities that would help you in meeting these needs. After each of the actions list the need or needs it might meet.

Action	Need(s)

MEETINGS AND GREETINGS

GOAL

To identify personal problem areas associated with social interaction.

FORMAT

Have participants complete the Meetings and Greetings checklist. Emphasize that the "other" space should be used for situations that are not covered by the general list.

PROCESSING

Poll participants to determine which situations are most problematic. Select one of these and ask participants to share what they actually do/say in the situation. Next have the group brainstorm some new approaches.

Meetings and Greetings

Listed below are a variety of social situations. Review the list and rate each of the situations according to the following scale.

0 = never a problem for me	1 = sometimes a problem
2 = often a problem	3 = always a problem

Think of "problem" in the sense of discomfort, apprehension, frustration, etc. the situation generates in you.

_____ First few moments of a job interview.

_____ Meeting your kids' teachers.

_____ Meeting your kids' friends.

_____ Phone calls with relatives.

_____ Meeting a new co-worker.

_____ Talking with a stranger seated next to you on a bus/train/plane.

_____ Small talk with your boss or other authority figure.

_____ Organizing/directing a group of friends to get involved with an activity.

_____ Breaking the ice at a get-together of spouse's co-workers/friends.

_____ Meeting a doctor/counselor for the initial visit.

_____ Talking with someone you haven't met before in a dining room or lounge.

_____ Meeting your new next-door neighbor.

_____ Meeting someone whose ethnic group or religion is different from yours.

_____ Meeting someone of the opposite sex.

_____ Small talk with your parents.

_____ Small talk with your kids.

_____ Small talk with your spouse.

_____ First time with a group/club you've joined.

_____ Other _____

_____ Other _____

INTRODUCTION INTERVIEWS

GOAL

To get to know the other members of the group.

FORMAT

This exercise provides practice at initiating and maintaining a conversation.

Each partner in a pair should take about five minutes to ask questions of the other to prepare an introduction of the individual to the group. Include the basics — name, interests, likes/dislikes, occupation, etc., but be creative in formulating questions that might provide novel/interesting information about the individual.

When participants are set with their introductions, they should spend a few minutes and work together on creating a cinquain. A cinquain is a five-line poem with specific information and number of words in each line. A form for creating a cinquain is shown on the following page.

PROCESSING

Have participants introduce one another and share their cinquains with the group.

Cooperative Cinquain

A cinquain has five lines with a specific number of words and specific topics on each line. An example would be

Toddlers

Active Unafraid

Moving Learning Changing

Happy Proud Tired Perplexed

Explorers

Work together to create a cinquain by filling in the lines in the table below. Some possible topics are music, fast food, nature, love, vacations, and volleyball.

Cooperative Cinquain

subject/object topic of poem	_____			
describing the topic, adjectives	_____	_____		
action occurring, verbs or phrase	_____	_____	_____	
how it makes you feel or what happens.	_____	_____	_____	_____
summary or synonym	_____			

20 (OR SO) QUESTIONS

GOAL

To learn about the leisure preferences of others and to share personal preferences.

FORMAT

Each participant is given a *20 Questions — Characteristics* sheet or a *24 Questions — What We Have* sheet (shown on the next two pages) and asked to complete it by questioning other group members. Participants can be given a time limit or minimum number of responses or people to talk to.

PROCESSING

Review the list, rotating among group members. Have members report who matched the particular characteristic.

20 Questions — Characteristics

This exercise is designed to get you to mingle — engaging in conversation with other group members and finding out more about them. The challenge is to answer as many of the questions as possible using as many of the group members as possible.

Find someone who matches each of these characteristics. You receive 1 point for each question answered and 1 point for each different group member identified. You have 20 minutes to complete the exercise.

Someone who...

- likes fast food _____

- considers themselves a Republican _____

- has grandchildren _____ How many? _____

- likes cats more than dogs _____

- has visited a foreign country _____ Where? _____

- enjoys classical music _____

- is more of a spender than a saver _____

- would rather live in the city than in the country _____

- listens to the radio or iPod more than they watch TV _____

- is pro-choice, believing that women should have the right to an abortion

  _____

- has played a musical instrument _____ What instrument

  _____

- roots for the Yankees _____

- has a hobby they enjoy _____ What? _____

- has won gambling money _____ What event? _____
  How much? _____

- was a Boy or Girl Scout or Scout Leader _____

- would prefer to live in a warmer climate _____

- has never gotten a traffic ticket _____

- reads more than two books each year _____

- does not want to lose weight _____

- thinks doctors are smarter than lawyers or engineers _____

24 Questions — What We Have

This exercise is designed to get you to mingle — engaging in conversation with other group members and finding out more about them. The challenge is to answer as many of the questions as possible using as many of the group members as possible. Find someone who has done each of these things. You receive 1 point for each question answered and 1 point for each different group member identified. You have 20 minutes to complete the exercise.

Some of us have...

- grandchildren — who _____ how many _____
- played sports in high school — who _____ what sport _____
- been to a National Park — who _____ what park _____
- worked as a waiter/waitress — who _____ where _____
- done volunteer work — who _____ for whom _____
- read the National Enquirer — who _____
- known someone named Amos or Andy — who _____
- been president or director of something — who _____
  where _____
- been to a summer camp — who _____ where _____
- been to an opera performance — who _____ what opera _____
- been to a professional wrestling match — who _____ favorite
  wrestler _____
- tried to cook Chinese food — who _____ what dish _____
- gone to the movies alone — who _____ what movie _____
- played a musical instrument — who _____ what _____
- maintained a friendship with a high school friend — who _____
  how long _____
- been a member of the YM/WCA — who _____ where _____
- seen the same movie five times — who _____ what movie _____
- run in a road race — who _____ when _____
- been on a blind date — who _____ how did it work out _____
- a hobby — who _____ what _____
- a garden — who _____ what's in it _____
- a really big TV — who _____ brand _____
- a Wii package — who _____ favorite game_____
- a joke we like to tell — who _____ joke _____

_____

EMOTIONAL LOTTO!!

GOAL

To identify some relationships between emotions and activities.

FORMAT

Participants receive an Emotional Lotto sheet and are asked to talk with other group members to fill in the blanks.

PROCESSING

Rotate among group members in sharing what they found for each of the responses. An alternative is to have each participant identify and report which of the nine areas is most "emotional" for them personally.

Emotional Lotto!!

Something That Makes Me Angry	**A Place That's Beautiful**	**My Favorite Month of the Year**
_____ Person	_____ Person	_____ Person
_____ Anger Producer	_____ Place	_____ Month
A Song That I Enjoy	**Happiest Day of My Life**	**The Best Thing About This Program**
_____ Person	_____ Person	_____ Person
_____ Song Title	_____ Day	_____ Best Thing
Someone Who Makes Me Laugh	**I'm Most Like a Roller Coaster, Bumper Cars, Merry-Go-Round, or a Giant Slide**	**An Activity that Lifts My Spirits**
_____ Person	_____ Person	_____ Person
_____ Laugh Maker	_____ Ride they're most like	_____ Activity

DREAMS AND SCHEMES

GOAL

To identify future leisure/lifestyle pursuits.

FORMAT

Have each participant complete the Dreams and Schemes sheet.

PROCESSING

Have each participant share the response that he or she is most excited about. An alternative is to choose one of the categories and ask participants to share their responses to it.

Dreams and Schemes

Place I'll Visit	Bad Habit I'll Stop	Skill I'll Acquire
Person	Person	Person
Where	Habit	Skill
Word Someone Will Use to Describe Me	House I'll Live In	Person/Group I'll Help/Reach Out To
Person	Person	Person
Word	Description of House	Person/Group
Group I'll Belong To	Accomplishment I'll Be Rewarded For	$ Lottery Winner Plans
Person	Person	Person
Group	Accomplishment	Plans
Sports Fantasy	Arts/Music Fantasy	Possession Fantasy
Person	Person	Person
Fantasy	Fantasy	Fantasy

COOPERATION AND TRUST SCALE

GOAL

To consider personal beliefs and attitudes concerning cooperation and trust.

FORMAT

Have each participant complete and score the Cooperation and Trust Scale.

PROCESSING

Have participants line up in order of their scores. As an alternative have them identify and share the item from the scale that they most strongly agree with and the item that they most strongly disagree with.

Cooperation and Trust Scale

Below is a set of questions that we would like you to answer honestly. By answering these questions and looking at your score, you will be able to learn more about yourself. There are no "right" or "wrong" answers.

Purpose:

The purpose of the *CAT* is to measure the degree of cooperation and trust that you feel.

Directions:

Listed below are 15 statements. To the left of each statement is a line for you to indicate how much you agree (or disagree) with the statement. Use the following responses:

1 Strongly Disagree   2 Disagree   3 Uncertain   4 Agree   5 Strongly Agree

_____ 1. Having a group's support makes many things easier to do.

_____ 2. Cooperation is important to doing well in school/work.

_____ 3. Employers think a cooperative attitude is important.

_____ 4. Cooperation is more enjoyable than competition in sports and games.

_____ 5. Helping others in enjoyable.

_____ 6. Trusting others is often a mistake.

_____ 7. Working as a team means taking orders.

_____ 8. Team sports and games are often frustrating because the mistakes of others can cause you to lose.

_____ 9. Showing compassion and caring for others is often not rewarding.

_____ 10. Working as a team means giving up your freedom.

_____ 11. A group can often produce results greater than those of any individual in the group.

_____ 12. Cooperation is important to making and keeping friends.

_____ 13. Taking risks is an exciting part of life.

_____ 14. Sharing is often enjoyable.

_____ 15. Success in the world is based more on your ability to cooperate than your ability to compete.

Score:

Add A____ + B____ + C____ = _____ total (average = 42)

A = #1 + #2 + #3 + #4 + #5

B = 30 - #6 + #7 + #8 + #9+ #10

C = #11 + #12 + #13 + #14 + #15

SOME UNIQUE PEOPLE

GOAL

To recognize the diversity and uniqueness of self and others.

FORMAT

Have participants complete the Some Unique People sheet by interviewing other participants.

PROCESSING

Have each participant share the most interesting thing he or she learned about someone else while completing the exercise. As an alternative have participants identify which of the areas they personally have a distinctive answer for.

Some Unique People

Likes, or at least tolerates, something which most people dislike	Has a stronger opinion than most people regarding a particular topic
_____	_____
Person	Person
_____	_____
Something	Topic
Has possession which few people have	**Has a talent or skill which few people have**
_____	_____
Person	Person
_____	_____
Possession	Talent/Skill
Been somewhere most people haven't	**Knows more about than most people**
_____	_____
Person	Person
_____	_____
Place	Subject
Has unusual hobby or interest	**Dislikes something which most people like**
_____	_____
Person	Person
_____	_____
Hobby/Interest	Dislike
Would appear next to this word if pictured in the dictionary	**Has read or watched something that many people haven't**
_____	_____
Person	Person
_____	_____
Word	Read/Watched

VIEW-ER CLUE-ER DO-ER

GOAL

To learn to cooperate with others in a group endeavor.

FORMAT

Working in three-person teams, the objective is to locate and retrieve an object (e.g., stuffed animal, ball) through cooperative effort.

The view-er is the only team member who can keep their eyes open during the activity. The clue-er is the only team member who can talk during the activity. The do-er is the only team member who can retrieve the object.

The activity begins with groups deciding on who will assume each role.

Teams are given a few minutes to plan a strategy for the activity. Remind participants that the viewer needs to communicate with the clue-er without talking.

To begin the activity the view-er and the clue-er stand about five feet behind the do-er. Let the groups know that the do-er is to remain in front of and separated from the other team members throughout the task.

When the groups are all set (only view-er has eyes open) the leader places the objects to be retrieved a distance away from participants and they begin the task of retrieving the object.

Repeat the activity with participants assuming different roles.

PROCESSING

Discuss which roles are easier and which roles are harder for each participant. Note that different people will prefer different roles because of their personalities.

ROLES IN GROUPS

GOAL

To understand that a person plays certain roles in a group and that the roles can change.

FORMAT

From the pairs of roles on the next page, have participants circle the role they most often take in this group.

Ask them to consider which role they are least pleased with and would like to change.

Tell them to work on the characteristics of their preferred role during the rest of the activities they are part of today.

PROCESSING

At the next group meeting, ask all participants how effective they were at changing their roles. What skills do they still need to learn? How could they have been more effective?

Roles in Groups

Consider the pairs of roles in the list below and circle the role you usually take in this group.

LEADER ----------------------------- FOLLOWER

FACILITATOR -------------------------- BLOCKER

COOPERATIVE----------------------- COMPETITIVE

RIGID---------------------------- COMPROMISER

ENTHUSIASTIC ------------------------- APATHETIC

SUPPORTIVE------------------------- DEGRADING

ACTIVE -------------------------------- PASSIVE

SERIOUS----------------------------- PLAYFUL

Choose one pair in which you're not pleased with your typical performance (e.g., too passive, too enthusiastic).

_____

During today's activities make an effort to monitor yourself concerning the characteristics and to be more of its opposite (e.g., if you feel you're too serious, be more playful). Write down where you succeeded and where you might need more skills to play the role you want to play.

POSITIVE ASSERTIONS

GOAL

To give and receive positive feedback.

FORMAT

Begin with an introduction focused upon the importance of being a consistent giver of positive feedback and a receptive receiver of the same.

Ask group members to relate an example of a positive assertion they've received, or have them identify one they would like to receive (e.g., you're a friendly person, you're a hard worker, you're a great bowler).

Next have each group member write their name on a piece of construction paper and secure the paper to their backs.

Challenge each group member to write a positive assertion or thought on every group member's paper.

PROCESSING

When this is completed, have each member review the feedback and share at least one comment with which they can agree or which meant most to them. Encourage them to state this using "I" language (e.g., I am a kind person).

A-Z

GOAL

To cooperate in meeting a goal.

FORMAT

Have a balloon and several balls available to conduct the activity.

Begin with the balloon or the beach ball and give the group the following challenge: the group needs to keep the ball in the air by tapping it (no catching allowed).

Every time someone hits the ball, he or she says the next letter of the alphabet. The group tries to get from A to Z without the ball touching the ground.

An individual can only have two hits at a time (it can come back to them later) and everyone must touch the ball at some point.

If you get to Z and someone still hasn't touched the ball, you can continue to say Z until you get it to everyone.

If the group is successful, challenge them with a ball that is more difficult to keep aloft.

PROCESSING

Discuss the group's feeling about requiring that everyone touch the ball and that only two hits in a row could be made by the same person.

THE RIGHT STUFF

GOAL

To practice organizing effective verbal communication and responding to questions.

FORMAT

Have each participant review the jobs listed on the next page and select the one in which they are most interested.

Ask them to prepare a brief statement describing their qualifications — without getting hung up on degrees, training, etc. — focusing instead on their personal characteristics/strengths, on why they should be hired.

Have each participant share his or her statement with the rest of the group.

Then have the group assume the role of an interview committee and ask the job applicant a few questions about his or her interest in the job.

PROCESSING

Group members should discuss how they felt about asking questions and answering them.

The Right Stuff

Review the jobs listed below and select the one in which you're most interested.

☐ Cruise director

☐ Greeter at a museum

☐ Gift shop manager

☐ Host/Hostess at a restaurant

☐ Counselor at a rehabilitation center

☐ Ride operator at an amusement park

☐ 4-H or scout leader or coach for youth sports

☐ Receptionist at a bank

☐ Library aide

☐ Self-serve gas station attendant

Prepare a brief statement describing your qualifications — don't get hung up on degrees, training, etc. Focus instead on your personal characteristics and strengths as you describe why you should be hired.

FEELINGS MENU

GOAL

To recognize feelings and understand it's possible to have some choice in how you feel.

FORMAT

Participants are asked to complete the Feelings Menu as detailed in the instructions.

PROCESSING

Participants share their Special of the Day and after each one is shared the rest of the group is polled to see if that's a feeling they also share. With the Choices section, ask participants to identify experiences or activities that tend to create that emotion for them.

Feelings Menu

Take a look at this Feelings Menu and write the feeling that best describes your current status in the blank under Special of the Day. If you have a feeling that's not on the list, feel free to use it.

Next select three feelings you would like to experience and write them on the lines under My Choices Today.

ANGRY	HAPPY	OPTIMISTIC	VULNERABLE
BORED	INDIFFERENT	PLAYFUL	WORTHLESS
CONFUSED	JEALOUS	QUARRELSOME	eXCITED
DEVIOUS	KIND	RELAXED	YOUTHFUL
EXCITED	LUCKY	STRESSED	ZESTY
FANTASTIC	MEAN	TIRED	
GUILTY	NAUGHTY	UNINHIBITED	

Special of the Day

_____

My Choices Today

_____

_____

_____

SURVEY

GOAL

To increase comfort level with asking questions.

FORMAT

Prepare some sample questions pertinent to a survey of interest to your group. For example, if the group was working on more effective communication they might ask:

- "What's the secret to being an effective communicator?"

- "What makes someone a good listener?"

- "What are the benefits and the liabilities of being assertive?"

Inform the group that they are going to be conducting a survey on a topic related to the group's focus. For example, if the group is concerned with teambuilding the topic might be effective teams.

Have the group generate prospective questions (e.g., What's the most important characteristic of an effective team?) and decide on two to four that you will include in your survey.

Set a time limit and have each individual interview one or two people outside the group using the questions the group has generated.

PROCESSING

When group members have returned, tally the answers they have received and summarize the findings.

CONTINUUM

GOAL

To express personal preferences and determine differences among group members.

FORMAT

Prepare a list of leisure/recreation contrasts pertinent to your group. For example, if you were working with a group of young adults you might include:

- Saver or Spender

- Morning Person or Night Person

- Artistic or Athletic

- Theme Park or National Park

- Country Music or Rock Music

- Dog Person or Cat Person

- Workaholic or Playaholic

Have the whole group stand next to one another.

Explain that the group is going to learn a little bit about each other by sharing where individuals see themselves on several contrasts.

Read the contrasts (e.g., Saver or Spender) indicating which side of the room is which and have participants move to where they feel they belong.

PROCESSING

Discuss any surprises about the choices group members made.

Discuss how it felt to have to choose which group to be in. Did they make choices based only on how they felt, or did they look to see what other people were choosing before they made their own decision?

WHO SAID IT

GOAL

To learn more about fellow program participants and to disclose information about oneself.

FORMAT

Have index cards and pens/pencils for each participant.

Inform the group that they are going to answer some questions and that their answers will be heard by the entire group.

Prepare 3-4 questions appropriate to your group. For example, with adolescents you may want to ask for:

- Something you're good at

- Favorite artist or group

- Job you'll have in 20 years

- What would you do with a million dollars?

Collect the completed cards and see if group members can identify who's who.

Read the answers on a card. If a group member thinks they know who it is they can say so (I think it's Jacob). If someone else agrees with the guess they can second it (Me, too).

Then ask Jacob if it's his card. If it is not a correct guess, keep the card in your pile and return to it later.

Continue until you've identified all the cards.

PROCESSING

Discuss how it felt to be recognized (or not recognized) by the answers you gave.

Stress Management

If you ask what is the single most important key to longevity,
I would have to say it is avoiding worry, stress, and tension.
And if you didn't ask me, I'd still have to say it.

— *George Burns*

Stress is a normal human response to change. We all experience it on a daily basis. Some stress in our lives can be good. For example, it can be a motivator to take action, to complete tasks on time, to perform, to accomplish developmental milestones, and even to get out of difficult or dangerous situations.

When you're watching an exciting sporting event, you're probably experiencing stress — but isn't it fun? If all stress were eliminated from our lives, we would also eliminate change. At first glance this may seem positive, but a life of total predictably and stability would likely result in boredom, which would introduce stress once more.

The point is we can't and shouldn't attempt to eliminate all stress from our lives, but recent literature suggests that unhealthy responses to stress and exposure to chronic stress can negatively affect physical and emotional health. Stress can weaken the immune system, making us more vulnerable to infections and inflammatory diseases. Stress has been linked to depression and anxiety and can contribute to relapse for those recovering from many types of addictions.

Therefore, as recreation therapists, it is important to encourage clients to manage their stress well in order to achieve optimal health. The activities which follow are designed to help you help your clients understand, manage, and optimize their responses to stress in order maximize their health and well-being.

REACTIONS TO STRESS CHECKLIST

GOAL

To help clients recognize positive and negative reactions to stress.

FORMAT

This is an introductory activity that will help clients identify how they respond to stress. Furthermore, it will help them begin to modify negative stress reactions.

Ask the client to complete the checklist on the following page.

Review the list identifying positive and negative responses to stress that your client currently experiences. The negative and positive response key is shown below.

Have your client circle negative responses to which they answered "yes."

PROCESSING

For each negative response, encourage your client to brainstorm ways to reduce or control negative stress reactions.

Reactions to Stress Checklist Answer Key

1. Negative	8. Negative
2. Positive	9. Positive
3. Negative	10. Positive
4. Positive	11. Negative
5. Negative	12. Negative
6. Negative	13. Positive
7. Negative	14. Positive

Reactions to Stress Checklist

Circle yes or no for each question below.

1. Yes No   Is it hard for you to get your mind off your worries?

2. Yes No   Do you prioritize tasks and tackle each one separately?

3. Yes No   Do you frequently feel tired?

4. Yes No   Do you share your feelings with family or friends?

5. Yes No   Are you prone to getting headaches?

6. Yes No   Do you feel really angry about minor problems?

7. Yes No   Do you feel inadequate or doubt yourself?

8. Yes No   Have your sleeping or eating patterns gotten worse recently?

9. Yes No   Do you have a balance between work and leisure in life?

10. Yes No   Are you able to say "No" to others?

11. Yes No   Are you highly critical of yourself and/or others?

12. Yes No   Do small pleasures in life no longer bring you satisfaction?

13. Yes No   Do you have ways to calm/soothe yourself when upset?

14. Yes No   Do you have an optimistic attitude toward life?

List some ways to reduce or control negative responses:

_____

_____

_____

_____

_____

_____

_____

_____

_____

_____

_____

_____

SOURCES OF STRESS

GOAL

To help clients identify and evaluate the sources of their stress.

FORMAT

This activity can be used effectively when working with individuals in a variety of settings including physical or psychiatric rehabilitation centers.

The idea is to help clients identify sources of stress in their lives that may be solvable or resolvable. In other words, we may have the power to eliminate or significantly reduce some stressors in our lives; those would be considered solvable. On the other hand, some stressors that may not be solvable can be dealt with in a more positive way; we can resolve to respond in a more positive way.

In this activity, you are not asking the client to come up with ways to solve or resolve their stressors. Instead, you asking them to identify and understand the sources of their stress.

Begin this activity with a discussion of what is meant by solvable and resolvable stressors.

Have the group members (or individual) brainstorm some examples for each source of stress.

Provide each client with worksheets shown on the following pages.

The first page asks the client to focus on the stressors that can be solved or eliminated.

The second page asks the client to focus on sources of stress that cannot be eliminated but can be dealt with more positively.

PROCESSING

You will want to point out that some sources of stress whether solvable or resolvable may require long-term efforts, while others can be dealt with in the short term.

In a supportive environment, having group members share responses can be very positive. Clients may gain insights and ideas from their peers.

Solvable Sources of Stress

Solvable Stressors (those that I can reduce or eliminate)

Relationship problems: _____

_____

_____

Burnout: _____

_____

_____

Problem job/loss of job: _____

_____

_____

Performance stress: _____

_____

_____

Environmental stress: _____

_____

_____

Boredom: _____

_____

_____

Lack of support: _____

_____

_____

Lack of money/resources: _____

_____

_____

Other: _____

_____

_____

Other: _____

_____

_____

Resolvable Sources of Stress

Resolvable Stressors (those that I cannot change but I can change my approach to)

Chronic illness or permanent injury: _____

_____

_____

Loss of a loved one: _____

_____

_____

Illness of a loved one: _____

_____

_____

Crime in the neighborhood: _____

_____

_____

Job change: _____

_____

_____

Move to a new environment: _____

_____

_____

Other: _____

_____

_____

Other: _____

_____

_____

Other: _____

_____

_____

Other: _____

_____

_____

PRESCRIPTION FOR MANAGING MY STRESS

GOAL

To assist clients in coming up with their own personalized method for managing stress.

FORMAT

This is a follow-up activity to Sources of Stress, the previous activity. Again, this is an activity that may be completed with clients on an individual basis or in a group setting. The benefit of completing this within a group is that clients can learn from each other's ideas.

It is important for the CLIENT to come up with a prescription for managing stress rather than the therapist. If a therapist or other group members attempt to prescribe a plan for another person, the plan will likely be met with resistance.

Review results from the Sources of Stress activity.

Share with the client information on the following page: Steps to Resolving Stress and Tips for Coping with Stress. The list of potential coping strategies is provided for clients to use although the list is in no way exhaustive. The more the client can personalize their coping strategies to their own personal situation the better.

Provide each client with copies of the worksheets on pages 151 and 152. These are duplicates of pages used in the Sources of Stress activity. However, now we are asking the client to look at ways to solve or resolve their stress.

PROCESSING

For items that clients have identified on their Solvable list, ask them to share their ideas on reducing or eliminating identified stressors. For items on the Resolvable list, ask clients to share their ideas on coping with stressors that cannot be eliminated.

Steps to Resolving Stress

Take notice of what is stressing you out. (Good news! You've done this!)

Pay careful attention to the details of this stressor.

Decide what your ultimate goal is.

Come up with some practical alternative for reaching this goal.

Act on your decision.

Evaluate the outcome.

Tips for Coping with Stress That Cannot Be Changed

Gain support from others who have been in a similar situation by joining a support group.

Treat yourself kindly and take care of yourself!

Make sure that you are getting adequate rest, exercise, and nutrition.

Surround yourself with positive people and positive images.

Keep a gratitude journal noting all the things in your life you are thankful for.

Do something kind for someone else.

Listen to music.

Involve yourself in meaningful leisure activities.

Practice relaxation techniques.

Express your feelings verbally and perhaps through art, music, writing, etc.

Resolve to have some fun each day.

Play with your pet.

Engage in something creative! Write! Paint! Sing! Rearrange the furniture!

Forgive yourself and others.

Get a change of scenery: go for a walk; take a trip; visit a place you've never been.

Focus on the meaning of your life. How might your current stressor actually enable you to positively impact others?

Incorporate laughter and humor into your day: watch a TV show that amuses you; read a joke book; watch a comedian; even forcing yourself to smile can reduce your stress level!

Try to view your stressor from a more positive perspective. Even though we can't change all our sources of stress, how we feel about them can make a big difference.

Prescription for Solvable Stress

Solvable: Practical alternatives that I can use to reduce or eliminate stressors

Relationship problems: _____

_____

_____

Burnout: _____

_____

_____

Problem job/loss of job: _____

_____

_____

Performance stress: _____

_____

_____

Environmental stress: _____

_____

_____

Boredom: _____

_____

_____

Lack of support: _____

_____

_____

Lack of money/resources: _____

_____

_____

Other: _____

_____

_____

Other: _____

_____

_____

Prescription for Resolvable Stress

Resolvable: Positive ways to cope with stress that I cannot change

Chronic illness or permanent injury: _____

_____

_____

Loss of a loved one: _____

_____

_____

Illness of a loved one: _____

_____

_____

Crime in the neighborhood: _____

_____

_____

Job change: _____

_____

_____

Move to a new environment: _____

_____

_____

Loss of independence: _____

_____

_____

Other: _____

_____

_____

Other: _____

_____

_____

Other: _____

_____

_____

A GIFT TO MYSELF:
MANAGING HOLIDAY STRESS

GOAL

To help clients recognize and prepare for holiday stress.

FORMAT

While most of us look forward to the holidays, they can also bring added stress to our lives. We often find ourselves trying to accomplish more in less time and with less money. This can also be a particularly difficult time for those who have recently (and even sometimes not so recently) lost a loved one. This activity encourages clients to focus on actions they can take that will help reduce holiday stress and increase levels of enjoyment. We often focus on gift giving during the holidays. This activity prompts clients to take action to prepare for holiday stress and ultimately give themselves the gift of an enjoyable season.

Begin this activity with a discussion about holiday stress.

Now pass out the handout found on the following page.

Have the client(s) discuss the following questions:

1. What is the most important aspect of the holidays to me?

2. When I think about previous holidays, what have been some of the barriers that make it difficult for me to truly enjoy the season?

3. Are there particular events that are difficult?

4. Above all, what do I hope to get out of the holidays?

PROCESSING

Ask clients to fill in as many boxes as they can with actions they can take to try to reduce or deal with barriers that interfere with enjoyment of the holidays. Encourage them to focus on steps that will help them achieve their overall goal for the holiday (question 4).

A Gift to Myself:
Managing Holiday Stress

POSITIVE SELF-TALK:
IS THE GLASS HALF EMPTY OR HALF FULL?

GOAL

To help clients recognize negative responses to stress and to practice substituting positive responses.

FORMAT

Of course the answer to this activity's title is "Both." The glass may truly be half full and half empty. However the way we view events in our lives, from a positive or negative viewpoint, can have an impact on our stress levels and our sense of satisfaction with life. Some negative thought patterns become second nature to us. This is an opportunity for clients to explore what negative responses are and practice using more positive responses. Several predetermined scenarios are provided. Additionally, clients, individually or as a group, can be challenged to come up with at least two scenarios in which they recognize that they feel stressed and in the past have not responded positively.

PROCESSING

Start this activity by asking the clients to provide the "correct response" to the question, "Is the glass half full or half empty?" It probably won't take much time for clients to conclude that the answer is both. But challenge them to take the next step and think about how point of view (negative or positive) can influence stress levels and a general sense of satisfaction.

On the following page, you will find an instructor's handout that includes events, examples of negative responses, and examples of positive responses.

Provide clients with the handout that includes negative, but not positive responses (next page).

Encourage clients to try to come up with positive responses that could reasonably be substituted for the negative responses.

You have the instructor's worksheet to use as a guide, but recognize that there are many appropriate, positive responses. Use your worksheet as an example. (There is no absolute right or wrong answer.)

There are two blanks at the bottom of the worksheet. Encourage clients to fill in the blanks with scenarios that have caused them stress in the past to which they have not responded positively. Alternately, clients can use the blanks to prepare for upcoming events that they anticipate will be stress producing.

Fill in the negative response that was used in the past.

Now encourage the client to substitute more positive responses.

Positive Self-Talk:
Is the glass half full or half empty?

Instructor's Copy

Event	Negative Response	Positive
Your supervisor assigns you a new task at work.	I'll never learn this.	This is a chance to learn something new.
It is afternoon and you find your time is running short for completing the work you planned to get done today.	There's not enough time.	I'll re-evaluate my priorities.
It looks like your money may run out before your month does.	I don't have the resources.	Necessity is the mother of invention.
A friend invites you to a party where he/she will be the only person you know.	I'll be too nervous to have fun. I'll stick out like a sore thumb.	This is a good chance to make some new friends.
You want to start an exercise program.	I probably won't be able to stick to it.	I'm going to look for an "exercise buddy" who can help me stick to it.

Positive Self-Talk:
Is the glass half full or half empty?

We've all heard this old adage: half full or half empty? The way we answer this question may reflect how we view ourselves and the world around us. Whether your outlook is positive, negative, or somewhere in between, your outlook influences how well you handle stress. This is a practice sheet designed to help you recognize positive and negative responses. In the left column, you'll see a list of possible events. In the middle column, a negative response is given. Try to come up with a positive response for each situation. You'll notice that there is room to add a couple of scenarios that you either know or can imagine that you might face in your life. Describe that situation, and then identify possible responses both negative and positive.

Event	Negative Response	Positive
Your supervisor assigns you a new task at work.	I'll never learn this.	
It is afternoon and you find your time is running short for completing the work you planned to get done today.	There's not enough time.	
It looks like your money may run out before your month does.	I don't have the resources.	
A friend invites you to a party where he/she will be the only person you know.	I'll be too nervous to have fun. I'll stick out like a sore thumb.	
You want to start an exercise program.	I probably won't be able to stick to it.	

THE PERFECT DAY

GOAL

To prompt clients to think about priorities in their lives and to conduct a reality check as to whether they are living out their priorities.

FORMAT

In some respects, we are all equal. We each receive 24 hours each day. And we will all die someday. However, many times we go through our days on automatic pilot, doing the things we think we have to do but ignoring the things that matter most. Engaging in the "busyness" of our life while ignoring our priorities can lead to stress and burnout.

One way to begin to evaluate whether we are living our lives the way we truly desire to is to describe the "perfect day." If given one day to live, how would you choose to spend that time? As noted in *Tuesdays with Morrie*, when you learn how to die, you learn how to live. In other words, recognizing that our time is finite can help move us toward living the lives we desire to live. While it is usually not feasible to give up all the chores required in daily life, we may be able to rethink the way we prioritize our daily activities in order to increase the congruence between "how I want to live my life" and "how I am living my life."

PROCESSING

Begin this activity by asking clients to describe a typical day.

Now ask them to describe a perfect day.

Now ask the question, "If this were your last day, would you make any changes?"

Give clients 20-30 minutes to create their perfect day. They can draw the perfect day or write about it if they prefer.

Have clients share about their perfect days if they are comfortable doing so.

Conclude by challenging clients to think of and share (if comfortable) at least one step they can take each day to make their perfect day more of a reality.

PROGRESSIVE MUSCLE RELAXATION

GOAL

To teach clients the process of progressive muscle relaxation and to let them practice that skill.

FORMAT

This is a relaxation exercise that is simple to do. It can be done with clients individually or in a group setting. The clients can learn this technique for use in their home environment.

PROCESSING

Conduct this activity in a quiet place that is free from distractions.

This activity is best conducted between meals—not right after a meal or close to mealtime.

Ask clients to get into a comfortable position, preferably sitting in a comfortable chair.

Clients can lie down during this exercise; however, lying down increases the chance of falling asleep which is not the goal of this activity.

Progressive relaxation is basically a two-step process. Going through separate muscle groups, the client tenses a muscle as tightly as possible and holds it for approximately eight seconds. The most challenging part of progressive muscle relaxation is isolating particular muscle groups. The ability to do so will improve with practice.

The second step is to relax the muscle. This should be a sudden letting go of the tension while exhaling. Focus on the feeling of relaxation, and maintain for approximately 15 seconds before moving to the next set of muscles.

Follow the above procedure of tensing and relaxing muscles going through these muscle groups, cueing the clients to tense and hold for eight seconds then release.

Right foot	Entire right arm
Right lower leg and foot	Left hand
Entire right leg	Left forearm and hand
Left foot	Entire left arm
Left lower leg and foot	Abdomen
Entire left leg	Chest
Right hand	Neck and shoulders
Right forearm and hand	Face

STRETCHING YOUR WAY TO RELAXATION

GOAL

To teach clients simple stretches that can help reduce stress.

FORMAT

This activity can be conducted individually or with a group. These stretches are designed to be done while sitting down, making them appropriate for people of all ages. The exercises can be incorporated into the workday and can be completed while sitting at a desk. Furthermore, these exercises can be used as part of a relaxation regimen or as a prelude to more strenuous activity.

PROCESSING

Begin by practicing deep breathing — breathe deeply in through the nose, then exhale through the mouth. Repeat 3-5 times.

While continuing deep breathing, begin stretching the following areas

Neck: While sitting up straight, turn your head and look to the right. Hold for six seconds and return to the middle. Now turn to the left. Hold for six seconds and return. Repeat this stretch to each side four times.

Neck: While sitting up straight, lower the right ear toward the shoulder. Hold for six seconds then return to upright position. Now lower the left ear toward the shoulder. Hold for six seconds then return to upright position. Repeat this stretch four times.

Shoulder shrugs: Raise both shoulders up as close to the ears as possible. Hold for six seconds then relax. Repeat four times.

Finger stretches. Make tight fists with hands in front of you. Hold for six seconds. Now extend the fingers out as wide as possible. Hold for six seconds. Now relax fingers and wiggle them. Repeat four times.

Arms and upper back: Lace fingers together, and extend arms straight out in front at shoulder height. Now slowly bring shoulders forward curving your back. Hold for six seconds then return to previous position. Rest for several seconds. Repeat four times.

Lower back: Start sitting up straight with knees together. Reach down over your knees and try to touch your toes (or shins, depending on your flexibility). Hold for six seconds and return to the original position. Repeat four times

Ankles and lower legs: Begin in sitting position with feet shoulder's width apart. Extend the right foot forward, maintaining contact with the floor while pointing the toes of the extended foot. Hold for six seconds. Extend the left foot forward, maintaining contact with the floor while pointing the toes of the extended foot. Hold for six seconds. Return to beginning position. Repeat four times.

Finally, raise your right hand straight above your head. Bend the elbow and allow your hand to drop down and touch your left shoulder blade. Now give yourself a pat on the back for taking steps to create a healthier, relaxed you.

MY LEISURE STRESSORS

GOAL

To identify and prepare for stress involved in leisure participation.

FORMAT

Getting involved in leisure activities is a great way to reduce your stress! However, sometimes certain aspects of leisure involvement can actually create stress. In this activity, clients evaluate and rate levels of stress associated with leisure activities. Finally, they are asked to brainstorm ways to reduce their leisure stress.

PROCESSING

Provide clients with the worksheet on the following page.

There are three scenarios listed that may induce stress for some people.

Ask the clients to rate their anticipated stress level for each scenario.

After each scenario, a space is provided for clients to write down ideas for reducing the stress associated with the scenario.

Now ask the clients to come up with their own scenario that might cause them to feel stressed.

Again, ask them to rate the level of stress associated with this activity and brainstorm ways to reduce their stress level without giving up the activity.

My Leisure Stressors

Scenario	Stress Level 1-10 (Low - High)	Ways to Reduce Stress
You recently moved to a new community. You've developed a friendship with a neighbor, and she invited you to a Tupperware party being held at her house. She says it will be a great way for you to meet some new people. You won't know any of the other attendees in advance of the get-together.		
You have decided that you would like to take up dancing as a way of getting some exercise and having fun. You've found a swing dance class that's offered once a week and you'd really like to try it. The advertisement says that all levels are welcomed, but you've never tried this dance before.		
You are a part of a Sunday School class. Every year, the class holds a special holiday dinner at one member's home. You have attended several of these get-togethers but you've never volunteered to have one at your house. You have enough space to accommodate the guests (approximately 25) and each guest will bring a potluck dish to share.		

Senior Activities

Grow old along with me! The best is yet to be.

— *Robert Browning*

According to *Healthy People 2010*, a primary goal of health promotion is to increase "quality and years of healthy life" (U.S. Department of Health & Human Services, 2000, p. 2). Individuals in the United States are clearly experiencing longer life; average life expectancy has increased from 47 to 77 years during the past century (The Centers for Disease Control and Prevention, 2007). The 85+ age group is the fastest growing segment of the population (U.S. Census Bureau, 2006). It is estimated that by 2020, 70 million Americans, or 20% of the population, will be at least 65 years of age (U.S. Census Bureau, 2006). However, as the goal of *Healthy People 2010* reflects, longevity alone does not necessarily equate with quality of life.

In our society, there is common anxiety and fear about growing older (Cummings, Kropf, & DeWeaver, 2000). As a society we tend to focus on negative elements of the later years and forget that this time can provide greater freedom and opportunity in the realm of leisure participation than in any other stage of life. At the same time, as people age, they are often required to face difficult transitions in areas of life such as housing, work roles, and relationships. Recreation therapists can utilize leisure education to help older adults embrace the opportunities that come with age and adjust to the challenges. The activities that follow are designed to help clients realize the potential that leisure involvement holds for improving quality of life while supporting well-being and development in times of loss and transition.

LEISURE SHOW AND TELL

GOAL

To help people become more comfortable with each other while focusing on leisure interests.

FORMAT

Leisure Show and Tell offers a new twist on a tried and true activity. At least to some degree, we all have a need to allow others to get to know us, to have our interests validated, and to get to know those around us. This icebreaker works well in a group setting. It can be used with clients of any age but has been especially well received by intergenerational groups. It's an activity that is useful during the first meeting of a new group.

PROCESSING

In preparation for a group meeting, ask all participants to bring to the group a favorite item that holds meaning for them and relates to their leisure interests. This should be an object/activity that they would feel comfortable sharing about with others in a group setting. Some ideas or examples may include a picture, a letter, a childhood toy, a craft, or a book.

If the group is larger than approximately 12 people, you may want to consider breaking into smaller subgroups.

Begin the activity with a little reminiscing about show and tell. Most people have participated in this activity in school, so encourage your clients to share a few remembrances on this topic.

Next encourage each person to take a turn sharing about their object with the group. The person should note how it relates to him or her and to leisure interests. Five minutes is usually plenty of time for each person.

Wrap up by asking participants about their experiences:

- Were there any things that you learned about others that surprised you?

- Did you find you had some common interests with other group members?

- Did you learn about an activity that you've never tried but you would be interested in?

WHO ARE YOU?

GOALS

To explore

1. how one's sense of identify develops over time and

2. the role that leisure may play in one's sense of who they are.

Working on these goals can be particularly helpful during times of transition.

FORMAT

Participants listen to a song that encourages them to reflect on who they are. Try to choose a song that the age group you're working with can relate to. The baby boomers, for example, may enjoy listening to The Who's version of "Who Are You" (The Who Album, 1978). An older cohort may enjoy "Sentimental Journey" (Brown & Horner, 1945).

After listening to a minute of two of the song, participants complete the exercise on the following page.

PROCESSING

Have the participants follow the boxes on the Who Are You? worksheet.

Have them begin at "Start" and move around the sheet, following the arrows and answering questions as they go. The prompts follow a chronological format.

Following completion of the activity, engage clients in discussion.

This activity may help people begin to look at their lives from a life-course perspective. You may encourage participants to look at how leisure interests have been impacted at different developmental periods.

For older adults transitioning into a new living situation, this activity may highlight that there are gains and losses (goods and bads) at every stage of life. They are entering a new stage, yet who they are today is made up of many of the choices and experiences that have occurred over a lifetime.

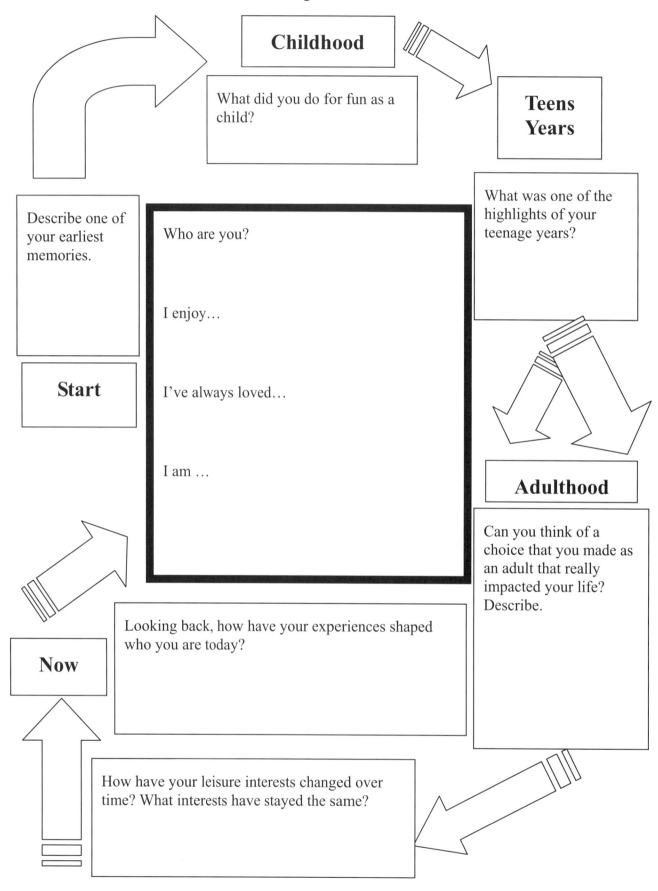

Childhood

What did you do for fun as a child?

Teens Years

What was one of the highlights of your teenage years?

Describe one of your earliest memories.

Who are you?

I enjoy…

I've always loved…

I am …

Start

Adulthood

Can you think of a choice that you made as an adult that really impacted your life? Describe.

Looking back, how have your experiences shaped who you are today?

Now

How have your leisure interests changed over time? What interests have stayed the same?

WHEREVER YOU GO, THERE YOU ARE...

GOAL

To become aware of leisure offerings in a new environment while working cooperatively with their peers.

FORMAT

Wherever You Go, There You Are... encourages people to begin to pursue leisure opportunities in a new environment by making them aware of activities that are available to them. It can be used in many settings. For example, this could be used in a hospital setting to acquaint patients with "free-time" activities, in a group home to orient residents to activities available within the home and in the surrounding community, or in a retirement community to familiarize older adults with activities available in this setting.

You will need to adapt the list of activities so that it fits the environment that YOU work in.

You can adjust the difficulty of this activity in several ways: place fewer items or more items on the list, make differences more or less obvious.

PROCESSING

Give participants a list of activities that are available to them in their current environment.

Divide participants into small groups of 3-8 (depending on functioning level).

Ask participants to work together with other group members to rank the activities in order given some kind of constraint (least expensive, closest, most calories burned, most time-consuming, etc.).

Here's an example that ranks activities by calories burned. It is tailored to residents who have recently moved into a fictitious retirement community called Leisure Ranch.

Following completion of this activity, have clients discuss the changes that they are facing and how their current environment differs from where they came from. Encourage clients to identify activities that are of interest to them which are offered in their current environment and to think about how they can begin to get involved now.

Activities ranked by calories burned[1]

206 calories, 30 minutes of swimming in our indoor or outdoor pool

206 calories, 30 minutes of tennis

184 calories, 30 minutes of gardening in the residents' garden

135 calories, 30 minutes of ping pong

---

[1] from http://www.healthstatus.com/calculate/cbc

135 calories, 30 minutes of biking on our bike trail

126 calories, 30 minute of beginner's Pilates class

117 calories, 30 minutes of golf on our 18-hole course (with cart)

117 calories, 30 minutes of strength training

94 calories, 30 minutes of walking at a leisurely pace (2 mph) on our paved trails

85 calories, 30 minutes of billiards

85 calories, 30 minutes of horseback riding

36 calories, 30 minutes of reading in the fully equipped library

Wherever You Go, There You Are...

Our facility offers A LOT of things to do! Check out the list below. Some of the items on this list may represent recreational activities that you are already involved in. Maybe you see some activities on the list that are unfamiliar to you — we hope you'll explore some new activities!

Staying in shape and engaging in meaningful leisure pursuits are important keys to optimal health. Finding the right balance of physical activity is an important part of this equation. Each activity listed below involves some kind of movement. And these activities can be part of your healthy lifestyle — starting now.

This is a group activity designed to help familiarize you with activities that are available to you at Leisure Ranch, as well as giving you a little more information about how many calories you will expend by being involved in them. Have fun!

Working with your group members, rank the 12 activities listed in terms of calories burned. Place a '1' by the activity that your group believes burns the most calories, a '2' by the activity that your group believes to burn the 2nd most calories and so on. End with the activity that your group believes burns the least calories.

The groups will be given 10 minutes to complete this task. The group with the most correct responses at the end of the 10 minutes wins...well, we all win when we get involved in healthy and enjoyable leisure activities!

Hint: There are four sets of "ties" in the list below, including numbers 1 and 2.

_____30 minutes of golf on our 18-hole course (with cart)

_____30 minutes of swimming in our indoor pool

_____30 minutes of strength training in our professionally staffed fitness center

_____30 minutes of tennis

_____30 minutes of ping pong

_____30 minutes of billiards

_____30 minute of beginner's Pilates class

_____30 minutes of walking at a leisurely pace (2 mph) on our paved trails

_____30 minutes of biking on our bike trail

_____30 minutes of gardening in the residents' garden

_____30 minutes reading in the fully equipped library

_____30 minutes of horseback riding (walking, not trotting)

LEISURE COAT OF ARMS

GOAL

To aid clients in leisure awareness.

FORMAT

Pride in family heritage has probably always existed but it appears to be more popular than ever these days, especially with older adults. You can use this point of interest to introduce the Leisure Coat of Arms.

Basically, the coat of arms is an emblem or pictorial description of a family, individual, or group of people. The images included on the coat of arms are symbolic of important traits, characteristics, or strengths of the individual, family, or group.

In this activity, clients are encouraged to complete their own Leisure Coat of Arms by identifying their leisure strengths and interests.

PROCESSING

It may be helpful to begin this activity with a brief "history lesson" on the origins of the coat of arms. A couple of websites that may be helpful include www.fleurdelis.com/meanings.htm and genealogy.about.com/cs/heraldry/s/heraldry.htm.

Provide individuals with the blank coat of arms. The coat of arms is divided into four sections.

There are four questions that correspond to the sections of the coat of arms. Provide a separate "question sheet" that the clients will use to complete the coat of arms.

Ask your clients to try to answer each of the four questions. They may write or verbalize their answers.

Next, have the clients complete the coat of arms sheet by drawing or using clip-art to fill in the four sections. For those who consider themselves to be "non-artists," remind them that the drawings should be simple. In fact, the simpler, the better. Stick figures are okay.

Have the clients put their names and the date in the sash at the bottom of the page.

Following completion of this activity, lead a discussion on how the clients define leisure, the role that leisure has played in their lives in the past and at present, how leisure can serve as a source of identity, and the positive benefits that leisure participation can create.

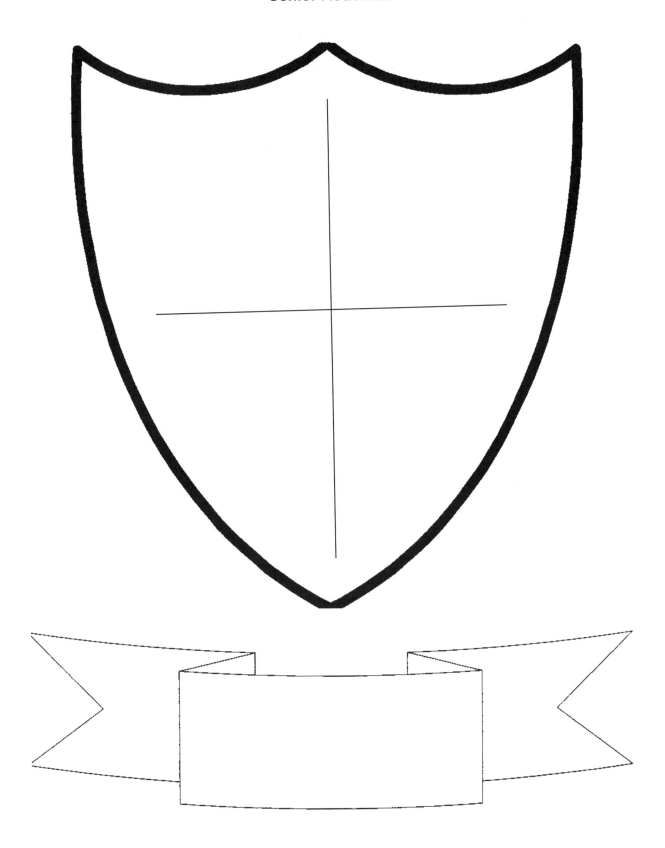

Leisure Coat of Arms Questions

1. Name a leisure activity that you enjoy or consider yourself to be good at. Have you always enjoyed this activity? Or is this a more recent interest?

2. Identify one leisure activity that you currently engage in or you would like to try that can help keep you healthy. How does this activity contribute to your health?

3. Thinking over your life, what was the MOST fun you ever had? What made it so special?

4. Name one event that you are looking forward to.

SUCCESSFUL AGING

GOAL

To educate older adults about the role that lifestyle choices and active engagement in life can play in overall health as one ages.

FORMAT

You may have heard the term "Successful Aging," but what does it really mean? In the past, if you reached your later years and were not sick, then you were considered to be doing well. We once thought that genes and family history were the biggest determinants of how we would age. But successful aging involves much more than not being sick. It means being as physically and mentally healthy as possible (Rowe & Kahn, 1998).

And as it turns out, our engagement in healthy behaviors is a bigger contributor to how we age than our family histories. In a book entitled *Successful Aging*, authors Rowe and Kahn tell us that successful aging involves maintaining three key behaviors: "avoiding disease, maintaining high physical and mental functioning, and engagement in life" (p. 39).

Leisure participation can have a significant impact on each of these areas and can contribute to successful aging. For recreation therapists working with older adults at any stage, *Successful Aging* is a great read.

PROCESSING

Clients will be asked to complete the following worksheet. Each item represents an aspect of successful aging.

In combination, these behaviors will help promote a high degree of physical and mental health.

Following completion of the activity, you may want to lead clients in a discussion of where they currently stand and ways they can improve their health and well-being.

- Are there activities that overlap and contribute to well-being in a variety of ways?

- How can the clients make the most of their leisure involvement?

Successful Aging Questionnaire

List leisure activities that meet the following goals. Try to list at least three activities in each section and indicate whether you are currently participating in each activity.

Leisure activities that help me avoid disease

Leisure activities that help me maintain high cognitive functioning

Leisure activities that help me maintain high physical functioning

Leisure activities that help me stay involved with other people and find purpose in life

THE CRYSTAL BALL: MAKING THE MOST OF YOUR RETIREMENT YEARS

GOAL

To assist clients in developing attitudes and behaviors that will contribute to their growth and well-being during their retirement years.

FORMAT

This activity may be useful when working with individuals who are getting ready to retire or who have recently retired. Retirement is viewed in variety of ways. For some, it is seen as a chance to rest up after years of intensive labor. For others, it may be seen as an opportunity to travel and engage in activities of choice. For some, retirement may be seen as a loss of identity with no formula for how one can or should structure their time.

As clients leave the workforce, it may be helpful to assist them in looking into their future and making appropriate plans. As recreation therapists, we can help clients develop positive attitudes toward meaningful leisure involvement and time management.

PROCESSING

It is helpful to have a "crystal ball" that you can use as a prop with this activity. Major discount and toy stores sell large (4") bouncy balls that are filled with a liquid glittery substance. This makes a perfect crystal ball. Have fun with it.

Explain to clients that as much as any of us would like to have one, no one actually has a crystal ball. For many people, retirement seems like an unknown. However, we can imagine what the ideal retirement would look like and begin to take steps to make the dream a reality.

Using a white/blackboard or posting large pieces of paper around the room, create several broad headings such as Hobbies, Volunteerism, Relationships, Post-Retirement Work, Health, Learning, Pace of Life…

Now pass the crystal ball to group members asking them to brainstorm ideas on qualities and characteristics of an ideal retirement. Record their ideas under the established headings.

After the brainstorming session, have each individual record three to five goals for creating their ideal retirement.

Have clients think about supporting factors and potential obstacles (finances, emotional support, availability of transportation, etc.). Given these considerations, do they need to modify their goals to make them more realistic?

Following completion of this activity, pass the crystal ball around the room once again, asking each person to share one thing they have learned or will take away from this discussion.

The Crystal Ball

Goals for creating an ideal retirement. Please list about five goals.

Supports

Obstacles

Revisions to Goals

BEEN THERE, DONE THAT: MAXIMIZING THE POSITIVE DURING TIMES OF TRANSITIONS

GOAL

To assist clients in recognizing their accomplishments and how coping strategies used in the past can be useful during current transitions.

FORMAT

Perhaps more than at any other time, later life is full of transitions. For example, in later life individuals may retire from a job, gain free time, change residences, lose a spouse or other loved one, develop chronic illnesses, lose income, remarry, gain grandchildren, etc. Change, whether it is viewed as positive or negative, usually involves stress. Fortunately, most older adults have developed effective coping strategies through life experiences. Recognizing these coping "successes" can be a way to help older adults maximize their ability to focus on the positive during times of transition.

PROCESSING

Have your clients think about some of the challenges they have faced in life. How did they feel during difficult times?

When looking at these challenges, what were some of the "success stories" — times when things turned out well? Describe the outcomes in detail.

Have the clients identify coping strategies used to deal with or overcome this situation. (Utilizing resources well, leaning on others, positive attitude, etc.)

Have the clients describe the transitions they are currently facing.

How do they feel about it? Are there any similarities to the way they felt when they were faced with challenges in the past?

Have the clients name coping strategies that have worked well in the past and can be applied to the current situation.

You may find the following worksheet to be a useful guide.

Been There, Done That

Some challenges I've faced in my life

Feelings at the time I was faced with the problem

Success stories

Coping strategies that worked before

Current transition

Feelings about the transition

Coping strategies that have worked before and might work now.

THE TIE THAT BINDS

GOAL

To help older clients recognize the value of social ties and to strengthen those relationships.

FORMAT

Older adults are likely to experience loss of social support through retirement, changing residences, death of a spouse, and death of friends.

Social support serves as a strong buffer for stress and contributes to health and well-being. Therefore, it is important to educate elders on the value of social support and to encourage strengthening those relationships.

PROCESSING

Begin the activity with a discussion on the importance of having relationships with people and the value that social support can offer. You may even want to encourage clients to think of the "most important" person in their lives and to share what it is/was that makes them so special.

Complete the worksheet on the following page.

Encourage clients to make a list of family and friends who are supportive and positive.

Have the clients list ways that these people support them (make me feel respected, always trustworthy, a listening ear, cheer me up, can confide in them, common interests, help me accomplish tasks).

Encourage the client to make a commitment to have meaningful contact in which they talk about things important to them with at least two people each day. Help them come up with a realistic plan of how they will stay in touch (phone, sitting together at meal times, email, letters).

Finally, assist the client in evaluating ways they can improve their support system if they are not satisfied with the support they currently receive.

The Tie That Binds

1. Make a list of family and friends who are supportive and positive.

Family

Friends

Neighbors

2. List ways these people support you.

Family

Friends

Neighbors

3. How will I stay in contact with my support people?

Family

Friends

Neighbors

4. Are you satisfied with the level of support you currently have? If not, how can you build your support system? (Some examples: join a new group, rekindle past relationships, join the foster grandparents program, volunteer, join a senior center or a support group)

MY WISH LIST

GOAL

To help older adults identify activities or goals that they have had on their list of things to do but haven't gotten around to doing. Taking that idea one step further, a goal of this activity is to encourage them to make realistic plans that will help make their goal a reality.

FORMAT

Part of development in late life is making peace with our life experiences. That can mean celebrating accomplishments and successes. It can also mean accepting failures and missed opportunities.

However, sometimes, there are items on our wish lists that lie somewhere in the middle of being an accomplishment and a missed opportunity — big or small. Here's an example to help clarify: You are working with an older man in an assisted living setting. He made his living as a farmer during his working years and retired from farming at age 65 when he sold his land and equipment. The farmer is now 86 and somewhat frail but is still able to ambulate independently with the use of a walker. Your client has identified as his wish the desire to take a tractor out in the field one more time. Your client has three children who visit regularly and are very supportive of your client. This activity would serve to help the client identify his wish in a concrete way and to start to take steps to make the wish a reality, if possible.

Keep in mind that it is not possible for all wishes to become reality, so as therapists, we may need to suggest alternatives or modifications.

PROCESSING

Ask each client to think about and perhaps share some of their accomplishments in life.

Now ask if there are leisure activities or leisure related goals that they have on their "wish list" but haven't gotten around to doing.

Encourage clients to attempt to identify at least one thing in their current environment and at least one thing in the community that they would like to do. This can be either an activity they would like to try or a goal they would like to accomplish.

The next step is to begin to make the wish a reality. Encourage your clients to make a list of steps that they can take to accomplish their wish.

Assessment

You can observe a lot just by watching.

You got to be careful if you don't know where you're going because you might get there.

In theory there is no difference between theory and practice. But, in practice, there is.

We're lost but we're making good time!

— attributed to Yogi Berra

The most important stage of planning and implementing a comprehensive leisure education program is the assessment stage. Through assessment, the practitioner gathers pertinent information from the individual in order to determine the nature and scope of the individual's leisure education needs. Information gathered through various assessment techniques can help to pinpoint any "problems" or "barriers" (real or perceived) that the individual faces in pursuing leisure experiences and opportunities.

There are a number of tools and techniques available to assist the practitioner in making an appropriate determination concerning an individual's leisure needs. It is not the purpose of this section to engage in a lengthy discourse or to recommend any particular assessment tools or techniques. It is rather to explore general areas that need to be considered in developing a comprehensive leisure profile of an individual. What follows is an outline of areas that ought to be targeted in the assessment process.

I. LEISURE HISTORY

It is important to recognize that individuals have had significant life experiences before service providers come in contact with them. It is necessary to obtain information about the individual's life experiences. Questions that can provide important information include

- What has the individual been interested and/or involved in?

- Are there any patterns evident as to the individual's leisure participation (e.g., active vs. passive, sedentary, self-initiated vs. dependent on others, etc.)?

Also, it is valuable to identify what type of lifestyle orientation the individual has acquired (e.g., strong work ethic, solo vs. group involvement, cooperative vs. competitive, etc.).

It is important to obtain an individual's perceptions as to the role of leisure in his/her life — past, present, and future.

- Does the individual view leisure as being utilitarian or diversional, etc.?

- Can the individual identify factors that influence his/her leisure pursuits (money, time, people, climate, seasons, work, family, etc.)?

- Is the individual's leisure influenced more by external factors (rewards, outcomes) than by internal factors (spontaneity, manifest joy, etc.)?

For the practitioner, the significant aspects that can be gleaned from an individual's leisure history are an understanding concerning the individual's leisure lifestyle patterns and an awareness of the individual's values and attitudes towards leisure.

II.   LEISURE PARTNERS

For most people, leisure experiences have meaning and value because those experiences are shared with other people. The social element is an important aspect to leisure. The second area to focus on is the social network of the individual.

- Who are the people that the individual affiliates with?

- How are they like the individual; how are they different from the individual?

- What are the characteristics of the individual's friends (age, gender, from the same neighborhood, etc.)?

- What type of relationships does the individual have?

- What is the average duration of those relationships?

- How frequently does the individual interact with friends, family members, etc?

- Are there factors that influence an individual's potential for establishing new relationships?

- Who are the people that the individual spends the most time with?

III.   LEISURE ASSETS

The next area to consider is the individual's leisure competencies.

- What are the leisure skills and abilities that the individual possesses?

- What are the things that the individual enjoys doing?

- What are the activities that the individual is successful at?

- Has the individual learned any new skills in the past year?

- Does the individual have an interest in learning any new skills?

- Is the individual involved in activities that are challenging — physically, emotionally, socially, intellectually?

- Can the individual perform activities that range the gamut from very simple to complex?

- What is important to note in this area — Are there any health related problems that might impact upon an individual's potential to learn new skills?

IV. LEISURE RESOURCES

Finally, it is important to obtain information concerning the individual's leisure resources.

- What is available at home, in the neighborhood, the community, the state, the region, and nationally that an individual can utilize to pursue leisure experiences?

That does not necessarily mean identifying just activities but also means identifying people, places, and things that can be helpful in pursuing leisure experiences.

Resource identification and resource utilization must go hand-in-hand.

- Does the individual actually utilize available resources?

Leisure Assessments

As previously stated, there are a multitude of tools and techniques that practitioners can and ought to utilize in assessing an individual's leisure needs. There is no single leisure assessment available that solicits the comprehensive information needed to plan an appropriate leisure education program. The practitioner must employ a variety of techniques such as observation and interview in conjunction with the various assessment devices in order to gain a full, clear, comprehensive understanding of the individual. *Measurement for Leisure Services* by Mounir Ragheb discusses these aspects in much greater detail. Examples of assessment categories/constructs include measurements of leisure involvement, leisure attitude, leisure motivation, leisure and free time boredom, leisure interests, leisure satisfaction, and playfulness and humor.

Idyll Arbor Leisure Battery (Ragheb & Beard, 1993)

Client ratings of statements on four scales measuring interest, attitude, motivation, and satisfaction.

Leisure Interest Measure

- Physical
- Outdoor
- Mechanical
- Artistic
- Service
- Social
- Cultural
- Reading

Leisure Attitude Measure

- Cognitive

- Affective

- Behavioral

Leisure Motivation Scale

- Intellectual

- Social

- Competence-Mastery

- Stimulus Avoidance

Leisure Satisfaction Measure

- Psychological

- Educational

- Social

- Relaxation

- Physiological

- Aesthetic

Leisure Step Up — Leisure Assessment (Dehn, 1995)

Checklist of opinions about the following areas:

- Leisure functioning

- Physical functioning

- Cognitive functioning

- Daily Living functioning

- Social functioning

- Psychological functioning

Leisure Step Up — Leisure Participation Level (Dehn, 1995)

Measure of the quality of leisure activities performed during a recent time interval. Based on an expansion of Nash's (1953) model of the leisure participation continuum.

Leisure Competence Measure (Kloseck & Crilly, 1997)

Therapist rating of client independence in the following areas:

- Leisure Awareness
- Leisure Attitude
- Leisure Skills
- Cultural/Social Behaviors
- Interpersonal Skills
- Community Integration Skills
- Social Contact
- Community Participation

Leisurescope Plus and Teen Leisurescope Plus (Schenk, 1997)

Determining leisure interests, emotional motivation, and need for higher arousal experiences through response to pictures of different types of activities in the following ten categories:

- Games
- Sports
- Nature
- Collection
- Crafts
- Art & Music
- Entertainment
- Volunteerism
- Social Affiliation
- Adventure

Personal Wellness Questionnaire (Bourne, 2005)

Response to a series of questions in the following areas:

- Exercise
- Relaxation
- Time management

- Stress management
- Sleep
- Nutrition
- Living environment
- Drug use
- Weight
- Appearance

Preferences for Activities of Children (PsychCorp, 2004)

Response to pictures identifying patterns and priorities in the following areas:

- What you like to do
- Jobs, chores, and employment
- Entertainment and education
- Active physical recreation
- Clubs, groups, and organizations
- Other skill-based activities
- Organized sports
- Quiet recreation
- Social activities
- Hobbies, crafts, and games

Your Brilliant Health Quotient: A Questionnaire (Foster & Hicks, 2008)

Level of agreement with statements regarding the following areas:

- Intention
- Accountability
- Identification
- Centrality
- Recasting
- Options
- Appreciation
- Giving
- Truth

Program Development

I thank you for having the courage
to affirm my need for joy and
inner peace, so neglected by others.
I thank you for recognizing that
more important than learning to walk
is discovering that there is someplace you want to go.

— Cathy O'Keefe
portion of a poem on behalf of clients
to providers of therapeutic recreation

Leisure education was practiced by American Red Cross and hospital recreation workers in the 1940s and 1950s. The basic idea that individuals affected by trauma, illness, or disability could utilize leisure and recreation activities to have more fulfilling lives has been a constant in the development of programs. Stumbo and Peterson (2009, p.42) describe leisure education as "a broad category of services that focuses on the development and acquisition of various leisure-related skills, attitudes and knowledge." In the context of a hospital stay, for example, leisure education can be as simple as learning to use the remote for the TV in your room, as profound as rethinking and making plans to retool your lifestyle.

Frames of Reference

There are many frames of reference in behavioral sciences that have relevance to leisure education. The three we've chosen relate particularly well to the three Rs model. With each program participants can assess their status, relate it to their personal situations, and make plans for change.

The first model is hardiness. Designed to define who best copes with stress (Maddi & Khoshaba, 2005), the model describes three factors critical for resilience — control, commitment, and challenge. Control, in contrast to feeling helpless and hopeless, has the obvious connotation of reflecting an individual's preferences and choices. Commitment is the antithesis of apathy. Things have meaning to you and you have passion for them: things as profound as your faith, as simple as your love of root beer floats or the Red Sox. Challenge has two aspects. The first relates to "flow" — a good balance of challenge, in the experiences you pursue, to your skill and competence level. Too much challenge and you're frustrated, too little and you're bored. The other aspect of challenge is your perception of change. Specifically, can you view change as an opportunity, not a threat? Helen Keller stated that when a door of possibility closed, another opened, but we didn't see it because we kept looking at the closed door. Taken together these three Cs form hardiness — a capacity to cope not mope when stress arrives.

A second model is Positivity (Fredrickson, 2009), an outgrowth of the positive psychology movement. A focus of this model is the notion of becoming well, not simply not sick — thriving and regularly perceiving positive feelings. The model encourages regular monitoring of the ratio of positive (e.g., serene, content, or peaceful) to negative (e.g., angry, irritated, or annoyed) perceptions. In addition to positive feelings, the literature detailing "authentic happiness" (Cherubini, 2009) describes two other constructs. Both are relevant to recreation and leisure — the "engaged" life (absorbed, in the flow) and the "meaningful" life (contributing to the community).

A third model is Likeability (Sanders, 2006). The process of likeability rests on an individual being friendly, relevant (they are a part of someone's life), empathic, and genuine. While it's unrealistic that everyone becomes a "Little Miss Sunshine," the notion that people can enhance their likeability and reduce their unlikeability seems possible and valuable to promoting friendships and positive relationships.

Program Components and Goals

The outlines below highlight six different perspectives on the "what," "how," and "why" of leisure education.

Avedon (1974)

- To strengthen existing social ties with individuals and groups, and to form new social ties

- To understand how to identify, locate, and use recreation resources

- To recognize the meaning of recreation in one's life

McDowell (1983)

- To resolve behavioral concerns

- To improve self-knowledge and understanding pertaining to leisure values, beliefs, and attitudes

- To match leisure interests with community resources

- To develop leisure-related skills and abilities that one lacks

---

Healthy Living through Leisure, Shank & Coyle (2002)

- Becoming informed

- Promoting competence

- Ensuring behavioral change

- Making healthy decisions about leisure

Dattilo (2008)

- To appreciate leisure
- To be aware of self in leisure
- To be self-determined in leisure
- To interact socially during leisure
- To use resources facilitating leisure
- To make decisions about leisure
- To acquire recreation activity skills

Stumbo & Peterson (2009)

- To demonstrate leisure awareness
- To display social interaction skills
- To demonstrate leisure activity skills
- To recognize leisure resources

Anderson & Heyne (in press)

- Well-Being: To experience a state of successful, satisfying, and productive engagement with life
- Cognitive: to think in a focused way and learn eagerly
- Physical: to do and act in daily life with vitality and no barriers
- Spiritual: to live life hopefully, in harmony with values and beliefs
- Social: to relate well to others and belong to valued social groups
- Psychological and Emotional: to feel happy and perceive control of one's life
- Leisure: to find enjoyment in leisure experiences and perceive that they positively impact other aspects of one's life.

Outcome measures of leisure education

We need ways to determine whether our programs are successful. The following is an example from Witman (1992) of what these measures of success could include in a clinical setting:

During Treatment

- Percentage of patients who recognize:
  - the relationship of personal needs and leisure potentials
  - barriers to leisure fulfillment
  - potential resources for fulfillment through leisure
- Percentage of patients who develop:
  - goals for future leisure
  - benefits/payoffs for accomplishment of goals
  - a plan for the accomplishment of goals
- Percentage of patients who evidence:
  - heightened participation/investment in other treatment
  - greater enjoyment/expressed satisfaction with treatment
  - commitment to aftercare goals and activities

Following Treatment

- Percentage of patients who:
  - are discouraged by length of stay
  - increase levels of leisure resource acquisition skills
  - are participating in recommended discharge leisure lifestyle program (at three months post-discharge)
- Percentage of family members/significant others who receive appropriate education and training regarding patients' community skills needs and who utilize such training.

Considering A-P-I-E

Following a systematic process for therapeutic recreation is seen as promoting competent, evidence-based, and client-centered practice (West, 2009). The following process — assess, plan, implement, and evaluate — can be used for leisure education. The process might best include:

Assessment that captures the client's story and provides personalized notions of strengths, wants, needs, and potentials.

Planning that identifies where a client's involvement is headed and how best to get there, and then establishes priorities, goals, and actions.

Implementation that considers both the content and process of experiences — activities, techniques, and environments.

Evaluation that is both summative and formative — identifying outcomes for clients and ideas for improvement of subsequent programming.

The 12 Warning Signs of Health

1. Persistent presence of support network.

2. Chronic positive expectations; tendency to frame events in constructive light.

3. Episodic peak experiences.

4. Sense of spiritual involvement.

5. Increased sensitivity.

6. Tendency to adapt to changing conditions.

7. Rapid response and recovery of adrenaline system due to repeated challenges.

8. Increased appetite for physical activity.

9. Tendency to identify and communicate feelings.

10. Repeated episodes of gratitude and generosity or related emotions.

11. Compulsion to contribute to society.

12. Persistent sense of humor.

From: Nathan, A. A. (2003). *The art of recreation therapy: Using activities as assessment tools.* San Francisco: Study Center Press, p. 39. (Original source listed as: Collected from bulletin board, Waldport, Ore: author unknown). Pulled from David Austin's RT blog in August 2010.

Websites

http://www.IdyllArbor.com/

Idyll Arbor is a publishing house geared toward recreational therapy professionals and students, activity professionals, and related professions. The primary focus of this organization is to provide resources and information that will support provision of optimal care to clients. Some publications that may be of particular interest include *Assessment Tools for Recreational Therapy and Related Fields, 4th Edition* (2010), *Measurement for Leisure Services* (2011), *Long Term Care, 6th Edition* (2011), the *Leisure Step Up* program for teaching about healthy leisure, and a variety of assessment tools.

www.venturepublish.com

Publications that may be helpful in developing a leisure education program include *Leisure Education I-IV, Activities and Resources for Leisure Education* by Norma Stumbo and a variety of leisure and social skill development materials. Two new texts scheduled for release in early 2011 focus on leisure education/facilitation techniques (Stumbo & Wardlaw, in press) and wellness (Anderson & Heyne, in press).

http://www.recreationtherapy.com/tractv.htm

Recreationtherapy.com provides a variety of information that can be useful to recreation therapists. It is not sponsored by or affiliated with professional organizations. However, information about professional organizations, salary rates, employment, and certification can be found. Note the leisure education activities listed on this page.

http://www.nmha.org/

Mental Health America is the largest non-profit agency in the U.S. designed to help people maintain positive mental health. In addition to a plethora of helpful information about mental health and disease, at this website recreation therapists will find a variety of activities that can be used in stress management and related groups.

http://www.realage.com

Real Age is a consumer-media health company that provides health information and health management tools. The site focuses on helping people live younger and healthier lives. The idea is that a lifetime of positive health behaviors adds up to a healthier aging experience. It's never too late or too early to get on board. This site has useful links that can be utilized in the provision of leisure education.

http://www.healthstatus.com/calculate/cbc

HealthStatus.com is a website designed to help people evaluate health status and health risks. There are 15 calculators and five health assessments that can be accessed from this page. This is the website used to determine calories burned in the activity Wherever You Go, There You Are…

http://www.ncpad.org/get/discoverleisure/

This website is a collaborative project of the National Center on Physical Activity and Disability (NCPAD), the National Center on Accessibility (NCA) and the Indiana University School of

Health, Physical Education, and Recreation. The resources available through this website will be particularly helpful for recreation therapists developing leisure education programs for children and youth.

www.theleisurelinkconsulting.com

This is the website of Alison Link that includes a variety of information about leisure and leisure education with a special focus on corrections and substance abuse.

www.deepfun.com

This is the website of Bernie DeKoven which includes a variety of resources for play and group development.

www.PositivityRatio.com

This website provides an electronic version of the Positivity Self Test.

Program Examples

This chapter provides examples of successful programs used in four settings: with seniors, in community reintegration, while teaching how to make better leisure choices, and in work with families. Activities used in the programs are shown after the program descriptions. Of course, you can use activities from the earlier part of the book in a similar program geared to the exact needs of your current set of clients.

Example 1: Leisure Education Program for Seniors

Audience

Older adults entering a retirement community

Outcomes

1. Participation in the community's recreation offerings

2. Development of friendships with other residents

3. Generating and acting on personal fitness goals

Session 1

Intro: Truth or Exaggeration? (description follows)

Main Activity: Virtual tour of programs and checklist

Wrap-up: Choose one to try and go to it before the next session

Session 2

Intro: People Bingo (example follows)

Main Activity: Games potpourri (variety of card and table games and puzzles)

Wrap-up: Share impressions and make a date for doing an activity with someone before the next session

Session 3

Intro: Fitness Facts (example follows)

Main Activity: Stretch demo and practice

Wrap-up: Develop a fitness contract

Truth or Exaggeration

GOAL

To learn more about other people in the group

PREPARATION

Give the group an example: think of two things that are true about you and one that is a "stretch" of the truth.

Have them vote on which one they think is the exaggeration.

IMPLEMENTATION

Have the group form teams of four to five people and have each team member share their two truths and one exaggeration with other team members.

Team members then guess which of the statements was the exaggeration.

After everyone has done this, have the team identify the individual whose exaggeration was most difficult to identify and have that individual present their two truths and an exaggeration to the entire group.

An alternative is to have the group generate and share two things that are true about all of them and one thing that is an exaggeration.

People Bingo

"B" in Their Name	"I" in Their Name	"N" in Their Name	"G" in Their Name	"O" in Their Name
Has Had a Broken Nose	Has a Pet	Collects Something	Fall Is Their Favorite Season	Is a Yankees Fan
Likes Jazz	Owns Stocks/Bonds	Born in May, June, or July	Saved a Piece Of Gum Overnight	Found or Won More Than $100
Likes Cooking	Likes Capri's	Likes Cats	Likes Pigs	Likes Classical Music
Has Been to a City/Town That Begins With "A"	Owns a Pair of Nike's	Been in an Auto Accident	Shot an Animal	Done Something Someone Dared Them To Do

Fitness Facts

True or False

_____ Exercise boosts brainpower.

_____ Exercise gives you energy.

_____ Movement melts away stress.

_____ Exercise lets you eat more.

_____ It's almost impossible to find time for exercise.

_____ Exercise causes many diseases.

_____ Exercise can weaken the heart.

_____ Relationships suffer when people focus on exercise.

Note: 1-4 are True, 5-8 are False

Adapted from "Top 10 Fitness Facts" by B.R. Sarnataro, http://www.webmed.com/fitness-exercise/guide/exercise-benefits

Example 2: A Note on Community Reintegration

By Angela Vauter, Jeff Witman, and Mary Ligon

Community reintegration can be an extremely valuable intervention choice for recreation therapists that can enable patients to attain competence and autonomy. It can provide a therapist and the treatment team with accurate data regarding skill performance. Entering the natural environment of the community challenges a patient's progress in therapy. One's adjustment to a changed condition (e.g., loss of mobility, ability to sequence tasks, anger control) can be accurately gauged by both the therapist and the patient.

The therapist now has a concrete example of the patient's status, and this experience enables the patient to better understand his/her actual strengths and needs. Goals can be adjusted or changed completely based on this reality experience. Community reintegration is a pragmatic approach to enabling a patient to have the needed life skills to successfully function in the community.

Goals

The goals of community reintegration are to provide clients with exposure to community resources and an opportunity to practice skills in a natural environment with the support of a therapist. Community reintegration also offers the therapist the opportunity to evaluate the client's skill level in a natural or non-clinical environment.

Specific Objectives

Community reintegration should occur only after patients have been assessed as ready for the experience and are prepared to maximize its potential through specific, agreed upon objectives. The comprehensive work of Armstrong and Lauzen (1994) in their *Community Integration Program* affords a systematic approach to determining readiness and purpose. The experience of going into the community can concentrate on application of skills, socialization, problem solving, and resource guidance. The critical component of environmental safety can also be addressed.

Processing

In general, community reintegration should be implemented under the following conditions:

- Physician's approval obtained
- Intervention identified on the treatment/care plan
- Staff/patient ratio determined and adhered to
- Written policy addressing community reintegration
- Careful staff decision on client's readiness for community participation
- Client's clear understanding of the purpose and goals of the intervention — verbally responds or communicates awareness

Following the experience, it is important to talk with the client about his or her perceptions of the experience. Items to discuss may include:

- How comfortable were you with this experience?

- Did you encounter obstacles or barriers to your independence that surprised you? If so, what were they?

- What skills do you feel you need to practice more in order to be more independent in the community?

Outcomes

Typical outcomes of participation in community reintegration include:

- Accurate self-assessment of skills by patient

- Accurate data for treatment team for evaluation of patient skills

- Knowledge of community resources and barriers

- Opportunity to practice skills needed to live as independently as possible

- Role modeling of desirable behaviors and interactions

- Practice for interactions with strangers in an uncontrolled (real) environment

Perhaps the most important process associated with community reintegration is planning. Checklists related to what's needed before, during, and after trips can ensure an experience in which learning takes place. Participants can focus on critical aspects of arrangements (e.g., Are any reservations required?), the experience itself (e.g., How can I best access the building?), and follow-up (e.g., Who's the best person to contact about architectural barriers I encountered?).

Facilitators too can focus on arrangements (e.g., What are the individual goals for the trip?), implementation (e.g., What if there's a medical emergency?), and processing (e.g., Which techniques will maximize participants' reflection on the experience?).

Subsequent experiences can provide opportunities to apply the answers to the questions being asked.

Example 3: Making Decisions Regarding Leisure Participation[2]

Jacqueline Cook, BSc, BScTR, CTRS

Recreation Therapist, Capital Health

Halifax, NS

Brief Description

The purpose of this session is to provide opportunities for participants to learn what they need to think about before participating in leisure. We will discuss what personal goals each individual has for leisure and look at how participating in the right activities can help achieve these goals.

Goal 4

Demonstrate ability to make decisions regarding leisure participation.

Objectives:

4.1 Identify personal leisure participation goals

4.2 Identify activities to achieve leisure goals

4.3 Determine requirements of activities identified to achieve leisure goals

4.4 Determine available personal resources needed for participation in activities intended to achieve leisure goals

Set-up for Room/Supplies

Ensure all of the chairs and tables are appropriately placed in a circle or rectangular format around the room to aid in group discussions.

Place materials such as pencils and workbooks (Appendix D) on the tables, and have the activities ready and organized.

Introduction

Content: Good morning and welcome to the Healthy Leisure, Healthy You series of leisure education sessions. My name is Jacqueline Cook and I am a Recreation Therapist here at Capital Health. For today's session, Making Decisions Regarding Leisure Participation, I will be talking about what participants need to think about before participating in leisure. We will discuss what personal goals each individual has for leisure and look at how participating in the right activities can help achieve these goals.

Process: Introduce session and myself.

---

[2] Part of a program of Leisure Education from Capital Health in Halifax, NS.

Welcome Activity

Preparation: Explain the activity to all the participants.

Content: We are going to start with an activity to get to know each other a little better. I want you all to think about a leisure activity you really want to try but haven't. I would like each of you to say your name and the reason you have never tried it.

Process: Use this game as an orientation activity. Explain to participants. Provide cueing and assistance as necessary.

Discussion

- Do you think you chose realistic activities?

- Do you think you will ever try it? Why or why not?

Objective 4.1: Identify personal leisure participation goals

1. Present concept of leisure participation goals

Content: Leisure has been loosely defined as:

- Time we are free to do what we want to do

- An attitude towards how you spend your time (you can hate that exercise class or enjoy challenging your body)

- Activity, involving intellectual or creative pursuits, physical activity, community service, socializing, and self-indulgence of plain old doing nothing (Hutchinson, 2010)

Process: Present information on defining leisure and what success is and how we can experience it in leisure.

A personal goal is something you want to accomplish or maintain. In order to meet goals we've made, we have to be willing to put effort into accomplishing them. Goals are important in personal growth and also in taking responsibility to create meaningful experiences. Developing goals in your leisure is the first step in the decision-making process leading to participation.

Making personal leisure goals is a process that requires energy and focus. Following through on these goals can be very rewarding. The following are some guidelines to help in the process.

- Your goals are your own. You are most likely to achieve goals you set for yourself than those set for you by others.

- Goals are clear, precise, and written. Writing goals can clarify them and make them more real. When goals are written, there is more of a commitment to accomplishing them.

- Some goals are accomplished in the short term. These goals are often attainable in a matter of days or weeks but give you the confidence to tackle larger goals.

- Goals are based on values. What you value will influence what is a priority for you to accomplish and the sense of fulfillment you will get when accomplishing them.

- Goals are realistic. Don't set yourself up for failure by setting a goal too high to reach. Start off with something small and work your way up. You know what you can accomplish. Stick to something attainable.

- Goals must be measurable. Your goals should be written so that you know when you've achieved them.

- Goals should have deadlines. Setting dates for your goals commits you to accomplishing them.

2. Discuss goals

- What is the value of determining your own goals?

- Have you ever written a personal goal before?

Process: Ask discussion questions and encourage all participants to engage in discussion. Use flip chart to write down the participants' responses.

3. Work through learning activity: Self-Contract (form follows program outline)

Process: Explain activity and give participants a few minutes to fill out the Self-Contract.

4. Discuss Self-Contract

Content:

- One by one share with us each of your goals.

- How successful do you think you will be?

- What have you learned about goal setting and decision-making so far today?

Process: Lead a group discussion using the discussion questions above.

Objective 4.2: Identify activities to achieve leisure goals

Content: Now that we've each set ourselves a goal, we will take this chance to look at what leisure activities will help us achieve those goals. There are often many activities you could do to achieve your goals. It is not necessary to do them all, but it is helpful to have many to choose from.

Process: Present information above offering examples as necessary. List key words on flip chart.

Objective 4.3: Determine requirements of activities identified to achieve leisure goals

1. Learning Activity

Content: Think about the goals you just set for yourselves. Now I want you to turn to the Get Ready activity and list as many activities in each category as you can think of that might help you achieve your goal.

Process: Explain activity. Divide participants into groups of three. List criteria for activity plan on flip chart.

2. Discussion

Content:

- Why did you choose those particular activities?

- How do the activities you selected help you to achieve your goals?

- How realistic are your selections?

- What did this activity tell you about your need to plan your leisure?

Process: Encourage all participants to engage in discussion using these questions. Use cueing and prompting as required.

Objective 4.4: Determine available personal resources needed for participation in activities intended to achieve leisure goals

1. Presentation

Content: Now we have several lists of specific activities that can help you attain the goal you set at the beginning of this session. Out of all the activities, select one activity you feel will help you attain your goal and you would really enjoy doing. Take a few minutes to fill out the Leisure Goal Setting worksheet.

2. Debriefing

Content

- Were you surprised by the amount of resources needed to participate in one leisure activity?

- Do you feel that thinking through these steps will help you reach your goals?

- What skills did you learn from this activity that you could use in the future?

Process: Conduct a discussion using the above questions. Encourage participants to contribute to the discussion.

3. Conclusion/Evaluation

Content: I hope you all enjoyed being here as much as I have. Thank you again for coming. I will see you on Wednesday.

Process: Conclude discussion and thank participants.

Leisure Activity Self-Contract

I want to achieve the following GOAL_____

1. What could keep me from reaching this goal?

____I don't have the skills, ability, or knowledge.

____Others don't want me to reach this goal.

____I don't want it badly enough to work for it.

____The goal is too difficult for me to accomplish.

____I'm afraid of what others might think.

____I don't have enough time, money, or other resources.

____I'm afraid I might fail.

____Other reasons:_____

2. What are some things I could do so that the concerns listed in question 1 don't prevent me from reaching my goal?_____

_____

3. Who can help me?_____

How?_____

4. What are my chances for success with this goal?

____Very good   ____Good   ____Fair   ____Poor   ____Very poor

5. Why do I feel this way?_____

_____

6. What are some good things that might happen if I succeed at this goal?_____

_____

7. What are some bad things that might happen if I succeed at this goal?_____

_____

8. What are the chances that bad things would happen if I reached the goal?

____Very good   ____Good   ____Fair   ____Poor   ____Very poor

9. What is the first step I can take to reach this goal?_____

_____

Self-Contract

I, _____, have decided to try to achieve the goal

          (Name)

of _____

by doing the following: _____

_____

_____

_____

My target date for reaching the final goal is_____.

Signed:_____Date:_____

Get Ready

I. Places to Go	II. Books to Read	III. Leisure Skills to Learn	IV. Things to Make or Produce
1.	1.	1.	1.
2.	2.	2.	2.
3.	3.	3.	3.
4.	4.	4.	4.
5.	5.	5.	5.
6.	6.	6.	6.

Leisure Goal Setting

1. Activity:_____

    a. What will you do?_____

    b. Does it require teaching or instruction?_____

    c. How long will you be there?_____

    d. How should you dress?_____

    e. How will you participate, with a group or as an individual?_____

2. Place/Location:_____

3. How to get there (transportation/directions):_____
   _____
   _____
   _____

4. When to go:

    a. Day(s) of the week_____

    b. Time of day_____

5. Cost:

    a. Entrance fee (per person or group)_____

    b. Equipment rental (or purchase)_____

    c. Transportation_____

    d. Food or refreshments_____

    e. Instructor's fee_____

    f. Other_____

    g. Total per visit_____

6. Supplies/Equipment needed:_____

7. Accessibility:_____

8. Other information:_____
   _____
   _____

Example 4: Leisure Awareness and Action Program (LAAP)

LAAP is a program focused on leisure and recreation for families. LAAP includes three modules:

- Playing Together

- Patterns and Possibilities

- Problems and Prospects

Playing Together

This component engages the family in cooperative play activities. Simple initiatives (Witman, 2008), parachute activities, and new games for families (LeFevre, 1988) are used as icebreakers. Discussion focuses on how people play, including frequency, level of involvement, and play styles. Parents are encouraged to share what they did for fun as children, and children are asked to anticipate what will be fun for them as adults. Knowledge of other family members' leisure interests is the focus of a Newlywed-Game-like family game. Children answer four questions, then their parents are asked how they think the children answered. Then the parents answer four questions and their children are asked how they think their parents answered. Points are awarded each time a guess matches the response. Family Game Questions (following this discussion) includes sample questions for both children and parents. Discussion focuses on how much participants know about their families and how to increase that knowledge.

Patterns and Possibilities

The second component begins with the construction of a leisure collage representing activities engaged in by various combinations of family members. For example, in a family group of three (mother, son, daughter), sections of the collage include the current activities of each individual and each of the combinations (e.g., mother and son). Another section is devoted to future activities. Discussion focuses on gaps in the current and future activity patterns (e.g., we don't do anything all together). Additionally, families consider various activity ideas (Krueger, 1988) and determine if they would be a good fit for their family. Finally, in a Leisure Lotto activity (following this discussion), family groups brainstorm then share their ideas on activities that could meet various needs.

Problems and Prospects

The final component involves families in activities related to expressed problems. Following the discussion there are brief descriptions of four typical activities (Mini Van, Straw Towers, Maze, and Pointer). Outdoor recreation activities, group initiatives, and low ropes course participation have also been used. How activities can be used regularly to help cope with problems is discussed. The families develop a contract specifying their commitment to a changed lifestyle. Families draft a letter to themselves detailing what they'll be doing for leisure three or six months in the future.

Note: See Witman & Munson (1992) for more information on the program.

Family Game Questions

For Children:

1. Dream date would be with _____.

2. Favorite fast-food restaurant _____.

3. Animal that's most like my personality _____.

4. Sport or game I'm good at _____.

For Adults:

1. Most often, during free time, I'm:

    - bored

    - angry

    - tired

    - wired

2. Number of states of the U.S. you have been in _____.

3. The best vacation for me:

    - mountains

    - theme park

    - ocean

    - big city

4. Favorite TV show _____.

Leisure Lotto

Fill in each of the spaces below with an activity that would meet the specified need for your family:

Make new friends	Refine skills or gain new ones	Get involved in the community	Be creative
_____	_____	_____	_____
Enhance fitness	Communicate better	Laugh, enjoy, and celebrate	Develop trust
_____	_____	_____	_____
Enhance spiritual connections	Try new foods	Relax and reduce stress	Strengthen old friendships
_____	_____	_____	_____
Make or build something	See new things	Help others	Experience an adventure/challenge
_____	_____	_____	_____

Mini Van

GOAL

To learn about trust.

FORMAT

Family lines up and places hands on shoulders of person in front of them. First and last person in line keep eyes open while middle people close eyes. Family (mini- van) moves around a designated course (or freely) with periodic stops to change positions until everyone has had a chance to be at each position. During the last stop the family is instructed to line up in any order they choose for a race among families.

PROCESSING

Focus on which positions people were most comfortable with, on willingness to keep eyes closed, and on why certain people were selected to lead final segment.

Straw Towers

GOAL

To improve decision-making and problem solving.

FORMAT

Families are given 50 straws and some tape and encouraged to build a self-supporting tower at least four feet tall. A ten-minute time limit is imposed with no talking during the first three minutes.

PROCESSING

How leadership emerged and how the group made decisions is discussed.

Maze

GOAL

To improve communication.

FORMAT

Entire group scatters around a room or along a walkway, becoming a human maze for a blindfolded family member to pass through. His/her family is challenged to use verbal instructions to lead the person through the group without bumping into anyone.

PROCESSING

Attention is focused on what made directions helpful or harmful and to what extent the whole family got involved.

Pointer

GOAL

To understand disclosure.

FORMAT

Families are seated in circles so that all are easily seen. The families are asked a series of questions. Immediately after each question is asked, each family member must point to the person who's their answer to the question. (They can point to themselves or to someone else.) Questions can include: In your family who's the a) best joke teller, b) most temperamental, c) biggest eater, d) best at doing chores, and e) worst at being on time.

PROCESSING

Review what was learned, surprises with results, and factors that might have kept you from pointing to your "true" answer.

A Final Thought

Man does not cease to play because he grows old,
Man grows old because he ceases to play.

— *George Bernard Shaw*

One of my father's favorite songs, which frequently was the background music for our suppers, can perhaps summarize the intent of leisure education programming. The song is the Guy Lombardo standard "Enjoy Yourself, It's Later Than You Think" with its reminder that the "years go by as quickly as a wink." So often we meet people who are in a rut of living for tomorrow, be it the weekend or vacation or that illusory paradise — retirement. Sacrifices of time, resources, relationships, and opportunities for enjoyment are inherent in this mind-set. Unrealistic expectations of our "future fun" may cause disenchantment when these experiences finally do arrive and fail to match our dreams of them. Like the bored elementary schooler who can't believe that the bell ending recess is ringing so soon, our greatest frustration may come with the realization that all our sacrifices were for something so transitory. The alternative — infusion of the spirit and experiences of leisure in our everyday lifestyles can be a difficult proposition. Even bad habits recognized as deleterious (for example, smoking or gambling) are difficult to break.

Among the most challenging habits or attitudes we confront in working with people in leisure education are

- the sense of resigned helplessness, of feeling controlled by people or environment or circumstances, which the person controlled sees no hope of changing;

- the sense of ennui, of being bored and tired and tired of being bored and bored with being tired and tired and bored of thinking how tired and bored we are and generally on a spiral in which everything becomes boring, tiring, or both (Stan Grabowski has described this as "dead from the skin in");

- the sense of aloneness, of being the only one unable to find pleasure in leisure, or make friends, or serve a tennis ball over the net, or to feel guilty about playing;

- the sense of being superfluous, of literally killing time with one's life, of not being a part of the big or any picture, of having no legacy except perhaps the desire of others to not be like you;

- the sense of complacency, of smugness and self-satisfaction with a lifestyle that even the casual observer can identify as not what it could be, or even as harmful.

Leisure education succeeds to the extent that it allows individuals to reject these attitudes and initiate habits that reinforce this rejection. Relatively modest trials of this exist within the sheltered environments in which we conduct programs. The true test of an individual's commitment to change comes in the real word. Without a supportive facilitator and group, people face their actual ability to evidence a changed lifestyle. Their success, it seems, relates in part to the attitude that the leisure education program leaves them with. It is probable that an enhanced sense of self-empowerment, the ability to both identify and solve problems, and the willingness to set goals are the critical legacy of involvement with leisure education programming. On a more basic level, we probably succeed to the extent that we instill and foster the four-letter word Philhaven staffer Ann Fisher describes as follows:

"We believe there is hope for everyone. It may be difficult to find and it may require help from others to get there, but it is well worth the search. Hope is often at the beginning of meaningful positive change and of a fully lived life."

The word is hope and with it comes the potential for reflection, recognition, and reaffirmation that makes a difference.

The 3 R's Crossword

Across

1. Full of fun

9. Renewed commitment

12. Avocation

14. Animating force

15. Life, liberty, and the pursuit of…

Down

2. Aficionado

3. Repose

4. Refreshment

5. A period of time devoted to R and R

6. Acknowledgement

7. Thought

8. Moxie

10. Trusting relationship

11. Ecstasy

13. Strain

References

Anderson, L. & Heyne, L. (in press). *Therapeutic recreation practice: A strengths approach.* State College, PA: Venture Publishing.

Armstrong, M. & Lauzen, S. (1994). *Community integration program.* Ravensdale, WA: Idyll Arbor, Inc.

Avedon, E. M. (1974). *Therapeutic recreation service: An applied behavior science approach.* Englewood Cliffs, NJ: Prentice Hall.

Bourne, E. J. (2005). *The anxiety & phobia workbook* (4th ed.). Oakland, CA: New Harbinger Publications, Inc.

The Centers for Disease Control and Prevention. (2007). *Health United States, 2006.* Retrieved January 28, 2007, from http://www.cdc.gov/nchs/data/hus/hus06.pdf#027.

Cherubini, J. (2009). Positive psychology and quality physical education. *Journal of Physical Education, Recreation & Dance, 80*(7), 42-47, 51.

Cummings, S. M., Kropf, N. P., & DeWeaver, K. L. (2000). Knowledge of and attitudes among non-elders: Gender and race differences. *Journal of Women & Aging, 12*(1/2), 77-91.

Dehn, D. (1995). *Leisure step up workbook.* Ravensdale, WA: Idyll Arbor, Inc.

Dattilo, J. (2008). *Leisure education program planning: A systematic approach* (3d ed.). State College, PA: Venture Publishing.

Fredrickson, B. L. (2009). *Positivity.* New York: Crown Publishers.

Foster, R. & Hicks, G. (2008). *Happiness and health.* New York, NY: Perigee.

Hutchinson, S. L. (2010). *Time for you: Learning to get the most from your leisure. Leisure education workbook.* Unpublished document. Halifax, NS: Dalhousie University.

Kloseck, M. & Crilly, R. (1997). *Leisure competence measure.* London, Ontario: Leisure Competence Measure Data System.

Krueger, C. W. (1988). *1001 things to do with your kids.* Nashville, TN: Abingdon Press.

Kunstler, R. & Daly, F. S. (2010). *Therapeutic recreation leadership and programming.* Champaign, IL: Human Kinetics.

LeFevre, D. N. (1988). *New games for the whole family.* New York, NY: Perigree Books.

Maddi, S. R. & Khoshaba, D. M. (2002). *Resilience at work: How to succeed no matter what life throws at you.* New York: American Management Association.

Mundy, J. (1998). *Leisure education: Theory and practice.* (2nd ed). Champaign, IL: Sagamore Publishing.

Nash, J. (1953). *Philosophy of recreation and leisure.* Dubuque, IA: Wm. C. Brown Company.

PsychCorp. (2004). *Children's assessment of participation and enjoyment.* San Antonio, TX: Harcourt Assessment, Inc.

Ragheb M. (2011). *Measurement for leisure services.* Enumclaw, WA: Idyll Arbor, Inc.

Ragheb M. & Beard, J. (1993). *Idyll Arbor leisure battery.* Enumclaw, WA: Idyll Arbor, Inc.

Rollnick, S., Miller, W. R., & Butler, C. C. (2008). *Motivational interviewing in health care: Helping patients change behavior.* New York: Guilford Press.

Rowe, J. W., & Kahn, R. L. (1998). *Successful aging.* New York: Dell Publishing.

Sanders, T. (2006). *The likeability factor.* New York: Three Rivers Press.

Schenk, C. N. (1998). *Instruction manual for Leisurescope Plus and Teen Leisurescope Plus.* Ravensdale, WA: Idyll Arbor, Inc.

Shank, J. & Coyle, C. (2002). *Therapeutic recreation in health promotion and rehabilitation.* State College, PA: Venture Publishing.

Stumbo, N. J. & Peterson, C. A. (2009). *Therapeutic recreation program design* (5th ed.). San Francisco: Benjamin Cummings.

Stumbo, N. J. & Wardlaw, B. (in press). *Leisure education and facilitation techniques in therapeutic recreation.* State College, PA: Venture Publishing, Inc.

U.S. Census Bureau. (2006). Dramatic changes in U.S. aging highlighted in new census, NIH report. Retrieved January 28, 2007, from http://www.census.gov/Press-Release/www/releases/archives/aging_population/006544.html

U.S. Department of Health and Human Services. (2000). *Healthy People 2010: Understanding and improving health.* Washington, DC: U.S. Department of Health and Human Services, Government Printing Office.

West, R. E. (2009). Integrating evidence into recreational therapy practice: An important focus for the profession. In N. Stumbo (Ed.), *Professional issues in therapeutic recreation: On competencies and outcomes.* (pp. 249-267). Champaign, IL: Sagamore Publishing.

Witman, J. P. (1992). An outcomes frame of reference for leisure education in therapeutic recreation. *Leisure Information Quarterly, 18*(3), 4-5.

Witman, J. P. (2008). *Taking the initiative.* State College, PA: Venture Publishing, Inc.

Witman, J. P. & Munson, W. W. (1992). Leisure awareness and action: A program to enhance family effectiveness. *Journal of Physical Education, Recreation and Dance, 63*(3), 41-43.

About the Authors

Jeff Witman, EdD, CTRS

Jeff Witman is Chair of the Behavioral Science Department at York College of Pennsylvania. Jeff's experience with the development and leadership of leisure education programs includes:

- inpatient behavioral health, drug/alcohol rehabilitation, and developmental disabilities programs;

- outpatient and day-treatment mental health programs;

- support groups for clients and for caregivers;

- a community-based program for seniors; and

- several alternative school, camp, and respite programs for children and youth with disabilities.

Academic influences on his development of leisure education programming include work with Chet McDowell at the University of Oregon (where Jeff got an MS) and Gerry Fain and Roxanne Howe-Murphy at Boston University (Jeff's doctoral school). He also credits his great aunt Mary Strickler Sarver, a Red Cross Recreation Worker during and after WWII, with fostering a passion for "teaching people to fish rather than just giving them the catch of the day!"

Mary Ligon, PhD, CTRS

Mary Ligon is an Assistant Professor in the Behavioral Science Department at York College of Pennsylvania. Mary is a Gerontologist who specializes in psychosocial development in late life, and she has been a Certified Therapeutic Recreation Specialist for more than 25 years. Mary has had the opportunity to develop and utilize leisure education programs in a variety of settings including: in-patient psychiatry, physical rehabilitation, and long term care environments.

Mary became acquainted with the concept of leisure education as an undergraduate at Radford University. Under the guidance of Gerald O'Morrow and Lee Stewart, Mary adopted the Leisure Ability Model (Petersen and Gunn, 1984) as a framework for service provision. Mary has used the concepts of leisure education in working with clients across the lifespan, promoting leisure involvement as a way of getting the most out of life.